THE XXL MEDITERRANEAN DIET RECIPES BOOK

Quick & Super-Delicious Dishes for Everyday Enjoyment | Secret Collection of Family Favourites | incl. Vegetarian, Snacks & More | with Nutritions

JAMIE HALLINGTON

© 2024 Jamie Hallington

All rights reserved

All rights for this book here presented belong exclusively to the author.

Usage or reproduction of the text is forbidden and requires a clear consent of the author in case of expectations.

ISBN – 9798338879771

TABLE OF CONTENTS

Introduction 9

Chapter 1: Breakfast & Brunch 10
    Greek-Style Scrambled Eggs with Spinach and Feta 11
    Avocado and Tomato Toast with Olive Oil and Sea Salt 12
    Lemon Ricotta Pancakes with Fresh Berries 13
    Herb-Crusted Halloumi and Grilled Asparagus... 14
    Shakshuka with Local Eggs and Tomatoes 15
    Frittata with Spinach, Tomatoes, and Goat Cheese 16
    Mediterranean Breakfast Pita with Hummus and Roasted Vegetables 17
    Tahini and Honey Toast with Chia Seeds 18
    Labneh with Fresh Herbs and Olive Oil 19
    Baked Eggs with Spinach and Tomatoes.. 20

Chapter 2: Starters & Appetisers 21
    Hummus with Roasted Red Peppers and Garlic 22
    Stuffed Grape Leaves with Lemon and Mint 23
    Courgette Fritters with a Mint Yogurt Dip 24
    Marinated Olives and Fresh Breads with Olive Oil 25
    Baba Ganoush with Pita Bread 26
    Grilled Halloumi with Lemon and Thyme 27
    Tzatziki with Cucumber and Dill 28
    Falafel with Tahini Sauce... 29
    Spiced Lentil Patties with Harissa Yogurt 30
    Caprese Skewers with Basil and Balsamic Glaze...................................... 31

Chapter 3: Salads & Sides 32

    Classic Greek Salad with Local Feta and Tomatoes 33

    Warm Lentil Salad with Roasted Root Vegetables and Tahini Dressing 34

    Charred Broccoli and Cauliflower with Garlic Lemon Dressing 35

    Bulgur Wheat Salad with Pomegranate and Fresh Herbs 36

    Fennel and Orange Salad with Olive Oil and Black Olives 37

    Grilled Aubergine with Tahini and Pine Nuts... 38

    Quinoa Tabbouleh with Fresh Parsley and Mint 39

    Mediterranean Potato Salad with Olives and Capers 40

    Roasted Carrots with Honey and Thyme...41

    Spinach and Orzo Salad with Feta and Lemon 42

Chapter 4: Main Courses – Vegetarian 43

    Aubergine Parmigiana with a Fresh Tomato-Basil Sauce 44

    Stuffed Peppers with Quinoa and Seasonal Greens 45

    Chickpea and Spinach Stew with Spices 46

    Mushroom Risotto with Fresh Herbs 47

    Vegetarian Moussaka with Lentils and Aubergine... 48

    Fennel and Potato Gratin with Parmesan 50

    Mediterranean Vegetable and Couscous Tagine 51

    Spaghetti with Fresh Tomatoes, Basil, and Olive Oil 52

    Spinach and Ricotta Stuffed Cannelloni 53

    Zucchini Noodles with Pesto and Cherry Tomatoes 54

    Stuffed Zucchini with Quinoa and Feta 55

    Aubergine Involtini with Ricotta and Spinach 56

    Stuffed Bell Peppers with Couscous and Feta... 57

    Butternut Squash and Lentil Curry 58

Chapter 5: Main Courses – Seafood.. 59

    Grilled Sea Bass with Lemon and Capers 60

    Seafood Paella with Local Mussels and Prawns 61

    Roasted Cod with Tomatoes, Garlic, and Olives... 62

Sardines with a Citrus and Herb Crust 63

Baked Salmon with Dill and Lemon 64

Prawns with Garlic, Chili, and Lemon 65

Octopus Salad with Potatoes and Capers 66

Tuna Steaks with a Sun-Dried Tomato and Olive Tapenade 67

Swordfish Skewers with Peppers and Onions 68

Clams in a White Wine and Garlic Broth 69

Chapter 6: Main Courses – Meat 71

Lamb Kofta with Mint Yogurt and Cucumber Salad 72

Grilled Chicken with Lemon and Thyme Marinade 74

Slow-Cooked Lamb Tagine with Apricots and Almonds 75

Spiced Meatballs in a Rich Tomato Sauce 76

Grilled Lamb Chops with Rosemary and Garlic 78

Chicken Shawarma with a Spiced Yogurt Marinade 79

Beef Souvlaki Skewers with Tzatziki 80

Moroccan Chicken with Preserved Lemons and Olives 81

Roast Pork with Garlic, Rosemary, and Lemon 82

Braised Beef with Red Wine and Thyme 83

Moroccan-Spiced Lamb Chops with Couscous 84

Stuffed Chicken Breasts with Spinach and Feta 86

Beef Kebabs with Garlic Yogurt Sauce 87

Greek-Style Lamb Meatballs with Tzatziki 88

Chapter 7: Desserts 90

Lemon and Almond Cake with a Honey Drizzle 91

Orange and Olive Oil Cake with a Citrus Glaze 92

Fresh Berries with Greek Yogurt and Honey 93

Baklava with Walnuts and Pistachios 94

Ricotta and Honey Tart with Fresh Figs 95

Poached Pears in Red Wine with Cinnamon and Star Anise 96

Lemon Sorbet with Fresh Mint 97

    Pistachio and Rosewater Ice Cream 98

    Almond Biscotti with a Hint of Lemon Zest 99

    Stuffed Dates with Almonds and Orange Blossom Water 100

Chapter 8: Preserves, Sauces, and Condiments 101

    Olive Tapenade 102

    Preserved Lemons 103

    Harissa Paste.. 104

    Homemade Tzatziki 105

    Pomegranate Molasses 106

    Tomato and Red Pepper Relish 107

    Romesco Sauce 108

    Basil Pesto with Walnuts 109

    Garlic Aioli with Lemon 110

    Tahini Dressing with Lemon and Garlic 111

    Spicy Red Pepper Hummus 112

    Roasted Garlic and Herb Butter... 113

    Chili Oil with Garlic and Herbs.. 114

    Sun-Dried Tomato Pesto 115

Disclaimer... 116

INTRODUCTION

> Bringing Mediterranean flavours into UK kitchens using local ingredients

The Mediterranean region is known for its rich culinary traditions, vibrant flavours, and a deep connection to seasonal, fresh ingredients. From the sun-soaked coastlines of Italy and Greece to the aromatic spice markets of Morocco and Turkey, the Mediterranean offers an incredible diversity of recipes that focus on simple yet flavourful ingredients. But what if you could bring these flavours to your own kitchen, using ingredients readily available in the UK?

This cookbook is designed to do just that—showing you how to recreate the magic of Mediterranean cuisine, all while incorporating fresh, local UK produce. From vibrant salads and hearty main courses to tangy sauces and indulgent desserts, every recipe in this book is rooted in Mediterranean tradition but tailored to what you can find at your local market. Whether it's substituting seasonal British vegetables, using locally-sourced seafood, or embracing the quality of regional dairy, we celebrate the balance between Mediterranean techniques and the bounty of UK ingredients.

In the following pages, you'll explore recipes that celebrate the essence of Mediterranean cooking: using the freshest, most flavourful ingredients, prepared in a way that allows their natural beauty to shine. With step-by-step guidance, you'll discover that cooking Mediterranean dishes is both approachable and rewarding, whether you're preparing a simple lunch or hosting an elaborate dinner.

So, grab your ingredients, embrace the spirit of Mediterranean cooking, and get ready to bring the sun-drenched flavours of the Mediterranean to your kitchen, all while supporting local farms and suppliers.

CHAPTER 1: BREAKFAST & BRUNCH

Mediterranean-inspired breakfasts that combine fresh vegetables, herbs, and grains with local UK produce.

GREEK-STYLE SCRAMBLED EGGS WITH SPINACH AND FETA

Fluffy scrambled eggs meet the rich, creamy flavour of feta cheese, complemented by fresh spinach for a healthy start to your day.

Portions: 2 | **Difficulty Level:** Easy | **Preparation Time:** 10 minutes | **Cooking Time:** 5 minutes | **Total Time:** 15 minutes

INGREDIENTS:

- 4 large eggs
- 100 g fresh spinach, roughly chopped
- 50 g feta cheese, crumbled
- 1 tablespoon olive oil
- 1 small onion, finely chopped
- Salt and pepper to taste
- 1 teaspoon dried oregano (optional)
- Fresh parsley for garnish (optional)

INSTRUCTIONS:

1. **Sauté the onion and spinach:** In a large non-stick pan, heat the olive oil over medium heat. Add the chopped onion and cook for 2-3 minutes, until softened and translucent. Add the spinach and sauté for 1-2 minutes until wilted. If using oregano, add it along with the spinach for extra flavour.
2. **Prepare the eggs:** In a separate bowl, whisk the eggs together with a pinch of salt and pepper until the mixture is smooth and well combined. You can add a splash of milk or cream to the eggs for a creamier texture.
3. **Cook the scrambled eggs:** Pour the egg mixture into the pan with the spinach and onions. Cook gently, stirring continuously, for 3-4 minutes, until the eggs are just set but still soft and creamy. Remove from heat. If you prefer firmer scrambled eggs, cook for an additional minute, but be careful not to overcook them.
4. **Add the feta:** Crumble the feta cheese over the scrambled eggs and stir gently to combine, allowing the cheese to slightly melt into the eggs. You can add more feta if you prefer a stronger flavour, or substitute with a mild goat cheese.
5. **Serve:** Transfer the scrambled eggs to plates and garnish with fresh parsley if desired. Serve with toasted bread or pita on the side. For a heartier breakfast, serve the scrambled eggs with roasted tomatoes or a fresh salad.

ESTIMATED NUTRITIONAL INFORMATION PER SERVING:
Calories: approx. 300 kcal | Fat: approx. 22 g | Carbohydrates: approx. 4 g | Fibre: approx. 2 g | Protein: approx. 20 g | Salt: approx. 1.2 g

AVOCADO AND TOMATO TOAST WITH OLIVE OIL AND SEA SALT

A modern Mediterranean twist on a classic favourite. Creamy avocado and ripe tomatoes come together on a toasted slice of bread, drizzled with high-quality olive oil.

Portions: 2 | **Difficulty Level:** Easy | **Preparation Time:** 5 minutes | **Total Time:** 5 minutes

INGREDIENTS:

- 2 slices of whole grain or sourdough bread, toasted
- 1 ripe avocado
- 1 medium tomato, sliced
- 1 tablespoon extra virgin olive oil
- Sea salt and freshly ground black pepper to taste
- Fresh basil leaves for garnish (optional)

INSTRUCTIONS:

1. **Prepare the avocado:** Cut the avocado in half, remove the pit, and scoop the flesh into a bowl. Mash the avocado with a fork until smooth, leaving some chunks for texture. For a creamier spread, add a splash of olive oil while mashing the avocado.
2. **Assemble the toast:** Spread the mashed avocado evenly over the toasted bread slices. Arrange the tomato slices on top, covering the avocado. For added flavour, drizzle a little olive oil over the avocado before adding the tomatoes.
3. **Season and garnish:** Drizzle the olive oil over the tomatoes and sprinkle with sea salt and freshly ground black pepper. For an extra burst of flavour, you can add a pinch of chilli flakes or lemon zest on top.
4. **Serve:** Garnish with fresh basil leaves if desired, and serve immediately. This toast pairs well with a side of mixed greens or a soft-boiled egg for a more substantial meal.

ESTIMATED NUTRITIONAL INFORMATION PER SERVING:
Calories: approx. 250 kcal | Fat: approx. 18 g | Carbohydrates: approx. 20 g |
Fibre: approx. 6 g | Protein: approx. 5 g | Salt: approx. 0.4 g

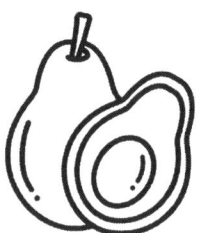

LEMON RICOTTA PANCAKES WITH FRESH BERRIES

Light and fluffy pancakes made with tangy ricotta and fresh lemon zest, paired with seasonal berries and a drizzle of honey.

Portions: 4 | **Difficulty Level:** Easy | **Preparation Time:** 10 minutes | **Cooking Time:** 15 minutes | **Total Time:** 25 minutes

INGREDIENTS:

- 250 g ricotta cheese
- 2 large eggs
- 150 ml milk
- 1 tablespoon lemon zest
- 2 tablespoons lemon juice
- 125 g all-purpose flour
- 1 teaspoon baking powder
- 1 tablespoon sugar
- Pinch of salt
- 1 tablespoon butter (for cooking)
- Fresh berries (strawberries, blueberries, or raspberries)
- Maple syrup or honey (optional)

INSTRUCTIONS:

1. **Preofpare the pancake batter:** In a large bowl, whisk together the ricotta, eggs, milk, lemon zest, and lemon juice until smooth. In a separate bowl, mix the flour, baking powder, sugar, and salt. Gradually add the dry ingredients to the wet mixture, stirring gently until just combined. Be careful not to overmix; a few lumps are fine.
2. **Cook the pancakes:** Heat a non-stick skillet over medium heat and melt the butter. Pour about 60 ml of batter per pancake into the skillet, spreading it slightly with the back of a spoon. Cook for 2-3 minutes, or until bubbles form on the surface and the edges are set, then flip and cook for another 2 minutes, until golden brown. For extra fluffiness, let the batter sit for 5 minutes before cooking.
3. **Prepare the berries:** While the pancakes are cooking, wash and dry the fresh berries. If you prefer sweeter berries, you can toss them with a little sugar or honey.
4. **Serve:** Stack the pancakes on plates, top with fresh berries, and drizzle with maple syrup or honey if desired. You can also dust the pancakes with powdered sugar for an extra touch of sweetness.

ESTIMATED NUTRITIONAL INFORMATION PER SERVING:
Calories: approx. 350 kcal | Fat: approx. 15 g | Carbohydrates: approx. 40 g | Fibre: approx. 2 g | Protein: approx. 12 g | Salt: approx. 0.6 g

HERB-CRUSTED HALLOUMI AND GRILLED ASPARAGUS

Crispy, golden halloumi cheese paired with tender grilled asparagus, flavoured with a medley of fresh herbs.

Portions: 4 | **Difficulty Level:** Easy | **Preparation Time:** 10 minutes | **Cooking Time:** 10 minutes | **Total Time:** 20 minutes

INGREDIENTS:

- 200 g halloumi cheese, sliced into 1 cm thick pieces
- 250 g asparagus spears, trimmed
- 2 tablespoons olive oil
- 1 tablespoon fresh thyme leaves
- 1 tablespoon fresh oregano, chopped
- Zest of 1 lemon
- Salt and freshly ground black pepper to taste
- Lemon wedges for serving

INSTRUCTIONS:

1. **Prepare the herb crust:** In a small bowl, mix together the fresh thyme, oregano, and lemon zest. Set aside. For an extra kick, you can add a pinch of chilli flakes to the herb mix.
2. **Grill the asparagus:** Preheat a grill pan or outdoor grill over medium-high heat. Toss the asparagus spears with 1 tablespoon of olive oil and season with salt and pepper. Grill for 3-4 minutes, turning occasionally, until lightly charred and tender. If you prefer softer asparagus, reduce the heat to medium and cook for an additional 2 minutes.
3. **Cook the halloumi:** While the asparagus is grilling, heat the remaining olive oil in a non-stick skillet over medium heat. Add the halloumi slices and cook for 1-2 minutes per side, until golden and crispy. Be careful not to overcook, as halloumi can become tough if left in the pan too long.
4. **Add the herb crust:** Once the halloumi is golden, remove from heat and immediately sprinkle the herb and lemon zest mixture over the hot cheese. For even more flavour, drizzle the halloumi with a little extra virgin olive oil just before serving.
5. **Serve:** Arrange the grilled asparagus and herb-crusted halloumi on plates. Serve with lemon wedges on the side for squeezing over the dish. This dish pairs wonderfully with a fresh green salad or a side of couscous.

ESTIMATED NUTRITIONAL INFORMATION PER SERVING:
Calories: approx. 300 kcal | Fat: approx. 22 g | Carbohydrates: approx. 4 g | Fibre: approx. 3 g | Protein: approx. 16 g | Salt: approx. 1.4 g

SHAKSHUKA WITH LOCAL EGGS AND TOMATOES

A warm and savoury breakfast of poached eggs in a rich tomato and bell pepper sauce, seasoned with cumin and smoked paprika.

Portions: 4 | **Difficulty Level:** Easy | **Preparation Time:** 10 minutes | **Cooking Time:** 20 minutes | **Total Time:** 30 minutes

INGREDIENTS:

- 4 large eggs
- 1 tablespoon olive oil
- 1 medium onion, finely chopped
- 2 garlic cloves, minced
- 1 red bell pepper, diced
- 400 g canned diced tomatoes
- 1 teaspoon ground cumin
- 1 teaspoon smoked paprika
- 1/2 teaspoon ground chilli powder (optional)
- Salt and freshly ground black pepper to taste
- Fresh coriander or parsley for garnish (optional)
- Crusty bread for serving

INSTRUCTIONS:

1. **Sauté the vegetables:** Heat olive oil in a large skillet over medium heat. Add the onion and bell pepper and sauté for 5-7 minutes, until softened. Stir in the minced garlic and cook for another minute, until fragrant. For extra depth of flavour, you can add a pinch of ground cinnamon along with the garlic.
2. **Add the tomatoes and spices:** Pour the diced tomatoes into the skillet, along with the cumin, smoked paprika, chilli powder (if using), salt, and pepper. Stir to combine and let the sauce simmer for 10-12 minutes, allowing it to thicken slightly. For a richer sauce, you can add a tablespoon of tomato paste.
3. **Poach the eggs:** Make small wells in the sauce with a spoon and crack the eggs into each well. Cover the skillet with a lid and cook for 6-8 minutes, until the eggs are just set but the yolks are still runny. For firmer yolks, cook for an additional 2-3 minutes.
4. **Garnish and serve:** Remove the skillet from heat and sprinkle with fresh coriander or parsley if desired. Serve the shakshuka hot, with crusty bread on the side for dipping. You can also top the shakshuka with crumbled feta for added richness.

ESTIMATED NUTRITIONAL INFORMATION PER SERVING:
Calories: approx. 250 kcal | Fat: approx. 14 g | Carbohydrates: approx. 20 g | Fibre: approx. 4 g | Protein: approx. 10 g | Salt: approx. 1.0 g

FRITTATA WITH SPINACH, TOMATOES, AND GOAT CHEESE

A fluffy frittata loaded with fresh spinach, juicy tomatoes, and creamy goat cheese. Perfect for a weekend brunch.

Portions: 4 | **Difficulty Level:** Easy | **Preparation Time:** 10 minutes | **Cooking Time:** 20 minutes | **Total Time:** 30 minutes

INGREDIENTS:

- 6 large eggs
- 100 g fresh spinach, washed and roughly chopped
- 100 g cherry tomatoes, halved
- 80 g goat cheese, crumbled
- 1 tablespoon olive oil
- Salt and freshly ground black pepper to taste
- Fresh basil leaves for garnish (optional)

INSTRUCTIONS:

1. **Prepare the vegetables:** Heat the olive oil in a medium oven-safe skillet over medium heat. Add the spinach and sauté until just wilted, about 2-3 minutes. You can add a small diced onion to the pan before adding the spinach for additional flavour.
2. **Make the egg mixture:** In a large bowl, beat the eggs with salt and freshly ground black pepper. Pour the beaten eggs over the wilted spinach in the skillet. Distribute the cherry tomatoes and crumbled goat cheese evenly across the top. For a fluffier frittata, add a splash of milk or cream to the eggs before beating.
3. **Cook the frittata:** Cook over medium heat until the edges begin to set, about 5-7 minutes. Then transfer the skillet to a preheated 190°C (375°F) oven and bake until the eggs are fully set and the top is lightly golden, about 10-12 minutes. Ensure the centre of the frittata is just set to avoid overcooking, which can make the eggs tough.
4. **Serve:** Remove the skillet from the oven and let the frittata cool for a few minutes. Garnish with fresh basil leaves if desired, and slice into wedges. This dish pairs well with a fresh green salad or roasted vegetables for a complete meal.

ESTIMATED NUTRITIONAL INFORMATION PER SERVING:
Calories: approx. 220 kcal | Fat: approx. 15 g | Carbohydrates: approx. 3 g | Fibre: approx. 1 g | Protein: approx. 16 g | Salt: approx. 0.8 g

MEDITERRANEAN BREAKFAST PITA WITH HUMMUS AND ROASTED VEGETABLES

Whole wheat pita filled with a layer of hummus, topped with roasted veggies for a simple, nourishing start to the day.

Portions: 4 | **Difficulty Level:** Easy | **Preparation Time:** 15 minutes | **Cooking Time:** 20 minutes | **Total Time:** 35 minutes

INGREDIENTS:

- 4 whole wheat pita breads
- 200 g hummus
- 1 red bell pepper, sliced
- 1 yellow bell pepper, sliced
- 1 zucchini, sliced
- 1 red onion, sliced
- 2 tablespoons olive oil
- Salt and freshly ground black pepper to taste
- 1 teaspoon dried thyme
- Fresh arugula for serving
- Feta cheese, crumbled (optional)

INSTRUCTIONS:

1. **Roast the vegetables:** Preheat your oven to 200°C (400°F). Toss the sliced bell peppers, zucchini, and red onion with olive oil, salt, pepper, and dried thyme on a baking sheet. Roast in the oven for 15-20 minutes, until the vegetables are tender and slightly charred. For additional flavour, sprinkle some garlic powder over the vegetables before roasting.
2. **Prepare the pita:** While the vegetables are roasting, warm the pita breads in the oven for 2-3 minutes or until they are just heated through. You can brush the pitas with a little olive oil and sprinkle with za'atar for extra flavour before warming.
3. **Assemble the pitas:** Spread a generous layer of hummus on each pita. Top with the roasted vegetables. Add fresh arugula and crumbled feta cheese if using. For a spicy kick, drizzle some sriracha or scatter a few chilli flakes over the top.
4. **Serve:** Cut each pita into halves or quarters and serve warm. These pitas are perfect for a hearty breakfast or a satisfying lunch.

ESTIMATED NUTRITIONAL INFORMATION PER SERVING:
Calories: approx. 350 kcal | Fat: approx. 14 g | Carbohydrates: approx. 45 g | Fibre: approx. 7 g | Protein: approx. 12 g | Salt: approx. 1.2 g

TAHINI AND HONEY TOAST WITH CHIA SEEDS

A quick and nutritious breakfast of toasted whole grain bread drizzled with tahini and honey, finished with a sprinkle of chia seeds.

Portions: 2 | **Difficulty Level:** Easy | **Preparation Time:** 5 minutes | **Total Time:** 5 minutes

INGREDIENTS:

- 2 slices of whole grain bread, toasted
- 2 tablespoons tahini
- 2 tablespoons honey
- 1 tablespoon chia seeds
- Fresh sliced banana or strawberries (optional)

INSTRUCTIONS:

1. **Prepare the toast:** Toast the bread slices to your desired level of crispiness. For an extra nutty flavour, you can lightly toast the bread with a brush of olive oil before applying the toppings.
2. **Apply the tahini:** Spread each slice of toast evenly with tahini. Ensure the tahini is well stirred beforehand to incorporate any natural oil separation.
3. **Drizzle with honey:** Drizzle honey over the tahini layer on each slice of toast. If you prefer a less sweet option, you can reduce the honey to 1 tablespoon or substitute it with agave syrup.
4. **Sprinkle with chia seeds:** Evenly sprinkle chia seeds over the honey. This will add a nice crunch and boost of nutrients. For additional texture and health benefits, consider adding a sprinkle of flaxseeds or hemp seeds.
5. **Add optional fruits:** If desired, top the toast with freshly sliced bananas or strawberries for extra freshness and a fruitier flavour. The addition of fruit not only enhances the taste but also increases the nutritional value.
6. **Serve:** Serve the toast immediately after assembling to enjoy the crunch of the toast with the creamy, sweet, and nutty toppings. This dish pairs well with a cup of green tea or a fresh fruit juice for a refreshing breakfast or snack.

ESTIMATED NUTRITIONAL INFORMATION PER SERVING:
Calories: approx. 300 kcal | Fat: approx. 15 g | Carbohydrates: approx. 35 g | Fibre: approx. 6 g | Protein: approx. 8 g | Salt: approx. 0.2 g

LABNEH WITH FRESH HERBS AND OLIVE OIL

Creamy labneh served with a drizzle of olive oil, fresh herbs, and a sprinkle of za'atar, perfect for spreading on toast or dipping with fresh bread.

Portions: 4 | **Difficulty Level:** Easy | **Preparation Time:** 10 minutes (plus overnight straining) | **Total Time:** 10 minutes active, overnight inactive

INGREDIENTS:

- 500 g Greek yoghourt
- 1 tablespoon salt
- 2 tablespoons olive oil
- 1 tablespoon fresh dill, finely chopped
- 1 tablespoon fresh mint, finely chopped
- 1 clove garlic, minced
- Fresh ground black pepper to taste
- Olive oil for drizzling
- Warm pita bread or fresh vegetables for serving

INSTRUCTIONS:

1. **Prepare the labneh:** Line a sieve with cheesecloth and place it over a bowl. Mix the Greek yoghourt with salt, then spread it into the cheesecloth. Cover and let it strain in the refrigerator overnight to remove excess whey and achieve a thicker, creamier texture. For a thicker labneh, you can let it strain for up to 48 hours.
2. **Season the labneh:** Transfer the strained labneh to a mixing bowl. Stir in the olive oil, dill, mint, and minced garlic. Mix well until all ingredients are fully incorporated. Season with fresh ground black pepper to taste. For extra flavour, you can add a zest of lemon or a pinch of crushed red pepper flakes.
3. **Serve:** Spoon the labneh into a serving dish and make a well in the centre with the back of a spoon. Drizzle additional olive oil over the top. For added visual appeal and flavour, sprinkle some za'atar or sumac over the labneh.
4. **Accompanying suggestions:** Serve the labneh chilled with warm pita bread or a selection of fresh vegetables like carrots, cucumbers, and bell peppers. Labneh also makes a great spread on sandwiches or as a creamy base for a savoury tart.

ESTIMATED NUTRITIONAL INFORMATION PER SERVING:
Calories: approx. 150 kcal | Fat: approx. 9 g | Carbohydrates: approx. 5 g | Fibre: approx. 0 g | Protein: approx. 12 g | Salt: approx. 1.5 g

BAKED EGGS WITH SPINACH AND TOMATOES

Baked eggs served over sautéed spinach and tomatoes, flavoured with garlic and a hint of chilli, a warm and comforting dish.

Portions: 4 | **Difficulty Level:** Easy | **Preparation Time:** 10 minutes (plus overnight straining) | **Total Time:** 10 minutes active, overnight inactive

INGREDIENTS:

- 500 g Greek yoghourt
- 1 tablespoon salt
- 2 tablespoons olive oil
- 1 tablespoon fresh dill, finely chopped
- 1 tablespoon fresh mint, finely chopped
- 1 clove garlic, minced
- Fresh ground black pepper to taste
- Olive oil for drizzling
- Warm pita bread or fresh vegetables for serving

INSTRUCTIONS:

1. **Prepare the labneh:** Line a sieve with cheesecloth and place it over a bowl. Mix the Greek yoghourt with salt, then spread it into the cheesecloth. Cover and let it strain in the refrigerator overnight to remove excess whey and achieve a thicker, creamier texture. For a thicker labneh, you can let it strain for up to 48 hours.
2. **Season the labneh:** Transfer the strained labneh to a mixing bowl. Stir in the olive oil, dill, mint, and minced garlic. Mix well until all ingredients are fully incorporated. Season with fresh ground black pepper to taste. For extra flavour, you can add a zest of lemon or a pinch of crushed red pepper flakes.
3. **Serve:** Spoon the labneh into a serving dish and make a well in the centre with the back of a spoon. Drizzle additional olive oil over the top. For added visual appeal and flavour, sprinkle some za'atar or sumac over the labneh.
4. **Accompanying suggestions:** Serve the labneh chilled with warm pita bread or a selection of fresh vegetables like carrots, cucumbers, and bell peppers. Labneh also makes a great spread on sandwiches or as a creamy base for a savoury tart.

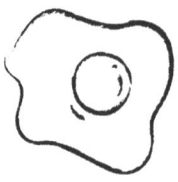

ESTIMATED NUTRITIONAL INFORMATION PER SERVING:
Calories: approx. 150 kcal | Fat: approx. 9 g | Carbohydrates: approx. 5 g | Fibre: approx. 0 g | Protein: approx. 12 g | Salt: approx. 1.5 g

CHAPTER 2: STARTERS & APPETISERS

Small plates perfect for sharing, showcasing Mediterranean dips, spreads, and small bites.

HUMMUS WITH ROASTED RED PEPPERS AND GARLIC

A creamy hummus base enhanced with the smoky sweetness of roasted red peppers and a touch of garlic.

Portions: 6 | **Difficulty Level:** Easy | **Preparation Time:** 10 minutes | **Cooking Time:** 5 minutes (if roasting your own peppers) | **Total Time:** 15 minutes

INGREDIENTS:

- 400 g canned chickpeas, drained and rinsed
- 200 g roasted red peppers, drained and chopped
- 2 cloves garlic, minced
- 3 tablespoons tahini
- 2 tablespoons olive oil, plus more for drizzling
- Juice of 1 lemon
- 1/2 teaspoon smoked paprika
- Salt to taste
- Fresh parsley or cilantro for garnish (optional)

INSTRUCTIONS:

1. **Prepare the hummus base:** In a food processor, combine the chickpeas, tahini, lemon juice, olive oil, and minced garlic. Blend until smooth. Adjust the consistency by adding a little water or extra olive oil if the mixture is too thick.
2. **Add roasted red peppers:** Add the roasted red peppers to the food processor along with the smoked paprika and a pinch of salt. Blend again until the peppers are fully incorporated and the hummus is smooth and creamy. For a spicier version, add a dash of cayenne pepper or a spoonful of harissa.
3. **Serve:** Transfer the hummus to a serving bowl. Drizzle with a little olive oil and garnish with chopped parsley or cilantro if using. Serve chilled or at room temperature with pita bread, fresh vegetables, or as part of a mezze platter.

ESTIMATED NUTRITIONAL INFORMATION PER SERVING:
Calories: approx. 190 kcal | Fat: approx. 10 g | Carbohydrates: approx. 20 g | Fibre: approx. 6 g | Protein: approx. 6 g | Salt: approx. 0.7 g

STUFFED GRAPE LEAVES WITH LEMON AND MINT

These tender grape leaves are stuffed with a savoury rice and herb mixture, finished with a squeeze of lemon and fresh mint.

Portions: 6 | **Difficulty Level:** Medium | **Preparation Time:** 30 minutes | **Cooking Time:** 45 minutes | **Total Time:** 1 hour 15 minutes

INGREDIENTS:

- 30 grape leaves, rinsed and drained
- 200 g cooked rice
- 100 g pine nuts, toasted
- 2 tablespoons olive oil
- 1 large onion, finely chopped
- 2 cloves garlic, minced
- 1/4 cup fresh mint, finely chopped
- 2 tablespoons fresh dill, finely chopped
- Juice and zest of 1 lemon
- Salt and freshly ground black pepper to taste
- Lemon slices for serving

INSTRUCTIONS:

1. **Prepare the filling:** Heat one tablespoon of olive oil in a pan over medium heat. Add the chopped onion and garlic and sauté until translucent, about 5 minutes. Add the cooked rice, pine nuts, mint, dill, lemon juice, and zest. Season with salt and pepper. Cook for an additional 5 minutes, stirring occasionally, until the mixture is well combined and fragrant. You can add a sprinkle of ground cinnamon for an extra layer of flavour.
2. **Stuff the grape leaves:** Lay a grape leaf flat on a work surface with the shiny side down and the stem toward you. Place a tablespoon of the filling near the stem end. Fold the stem end over the filling, then fold both sides toward the middle, and roll tightly into a cylinder. Repeat with the remaining grape leaves and filling. Ensure the rolls are tight enough to hold the filling but allow some room for the rice to expand.
3. **Cook the grape leaves:** Arrange the stuffed grape leaves in a large pot in tight layers. Drizzle with the remaining olive oil and cover with a layer of lemon slices. Add enough water to just cover the grape leaves. Place an inverted plate on top of the grape leaves to keep them submerged. Bring to a simmer over medium heat, reduce to low, and cook for 40 minutes, until the grape leaves are tender and the filling is heated through.
4. **Serve:** Allow the grape leaves to cool slightly in the pot before serving. Serve warm or at room temperature, garnished with extra lemon slices.

ESTIMATED NUTRITIONAL INFORMATION PER SERVING:
Calories: approx. 180 kcal | Fat: approx. 10 g | Carbohydrates: approx. 20 g | Fibre: approx. 3 g | Protein: approx. 4 g | Salt: approx. 0.8 g

COURGETTE FRITTERS WITH A MINT YOGURT DIP

Crispy on the outside and soft on the inside, these courgette fritters are bursting with fresh flavours.

Portions: 4 | **Difficulty Level:** Easy | **Preparation Time:** 15 minutes | **Cooking Time:** 10 minutes | **Total Time:** 25 minutes

INGREDIENTS:

- 3 medium courgettes (zucchini), grated
- 1 small onion, finely chopped
- 2 cloves garlic, minced
- 100 g feta cheese, crumbled
- 1 large egg, beaten
- 75 g all-purpose flour
- 1/2 teaspoon baking powder
- Salt and freshly ground black pepper to taste
- Olive oil for frying

For the Mint Yogurt Dip:
- 200 g Greek yoghourt
- 2 tablespoons fresh mint, finely chopped
- 1 tablespoon lemon juice
- Salt to taste

INSTRUCTIONS:

1. **Prepare the courgette mixture:** Place the grated courgettes in a colander, sprinkle with a little salt, and let sit for 10 minutes to draw out moisture. Squeeze the excess water from the courgettes using a clean dish towel. Transfer to a mixing bowl and add the onion, garlic, crumbled feta, and beaten egg. Stir to combine.
2. **Make the fritter batter:** Add the flour and baking powder to the courgette mixture and season with black pepper. Mix until well combined. The mixture should be thick enough to hold its shape when scooped. If the mixture is too wet, add a little more flour to achieve the desired consistency.
3. **Cook the fritters:** Heat a thin layer of olive oil in a large skillet over medium heat. Drop heaped tablespoons of the batter into the skillet, flattening slightly with the back of the spoon to form round fritters. Fry for about 2-3 minutes on each side or until golden brown and cooked through. Do not overcrowd the pan; cook in batches if necessary.
4. **Prepare the mint yoghourt dip:** While the fritters are cooking, combine the Greek yoghourt, chopped mint, and lemon juice in a small bowl. Season with salt to taste and stir until smooth. For an extra refreshing touch, add a pinch of lemon zest to the dip.
5. **Serve:** Serve the warm courgette fritters immediately with the mint yoghourt dip on the side. These fritters are perfect as a light meal or can be served as an appetiser for guests.

ESTIMATED NUTRITIONAL INFORMATION PER SERVING:
Calories: approx. 250 kcal | Fat: approx. 15 g | Carbohydrates: approx. 20 g | Fibre: approx. 2 g | Protein: approx. 9 g | Salt: approx. 0.7 g

MARINATED OLIVES AND FRESH BREADS WITH OLIVE OIL

Marinated olives infused with Mediterranean herbs and citrus, served alongside fresh bread for dipping into extra virgin olive oil.

Portions: 4 | **Difficulty Level:** Easy | **Preparation Time:** 10 minutes + marinating time | **Total Time:** 10 minutes (excluding marinating time)

INGREDIENTS:
- 300 g mixed olives (e.g., Kalamata, green, black)
- 3 cloves garlic, thinly sliced
- 1 small orange, zest and juice
- 2 tablespoons fresh rosemary, chopped
- 2 tablespoons fresh thyme, chopped
- 1/4 cup extra virgin olive oil, plus more for serving
- Freshly ground black pepper to taste
- Artisan bread, for serving

INSTRUCTIONS:
1. **Marinate the olives:** In a medium bowl, combine the olives, garlic slices, orange zest and juice, chopped rosemary, and thyme. Pour over the olive oil and toss gently to coat. Season with freshly ground black pepper. Cover and let marinate in the refrigerator for at least 2 hours, preferably overnight, to allow the flavours to meld. For a spicy twist, add a pinch of red chilli flakes.
2. **Prepare the bread:** When ready to serve, slice the artisan bread and lightly toast it, if desired. Drizzle some olive oil on the bread before toasting for added flavour.
3. **Serve:** Arrange the marinated olives in a serving dish and place the toasted bread alongside. Drizzle both the olives and the bread with additional olive oil right before serving. Garnish with additional herbs if desired to enhance the presentation.

ESTIMATED NUTRITIONAL INFORMATION PER SERVING:
Calories: approx. 200 kcal | Fat: approx. 18 g | Carbohydrates: approx. 8 g | Fibre: approx. 3 g | Protein: approx. 2 g | Salt: approx. 1.0 g

BABA GANOUSH WITH PITA BREAD

A smoky eggplant dip, made smooth and creamy with tahini and garlic. Perfect for spreading on pita bread.

Portions: 4 | **Difficulty Level:** Easy | **Preparation Time:** 15 minutes | **Cooking Time:** 30 minutes | **Total Time:** 45 minutes

INGREDIENTS:

- 2 large eggplants
- 3 tablespoons tahini
- 2 cloves garlic, minced
- Juice of 1 lemon
- 2 tablespoons olive oil, plus more for drizzling
- Salt and freshly ground black pepper to taste
- 1 tablespoon fresh parsley, chopped (for garnish)
- Pita bread, for serving

INSTRUCTIONS:

1. **Roast the eggplants:** Preheat your oven to 200°C (400°F). Pierce the eggplants with a fork and place them on a baking sheet. Roast in the oven for 30-35 minutes, turning occasionally, until the skin is charred and the insides are tender. You can also grill the eggplants over open flame for a smokier flavour.
2. **Prepare the baba ganoush:** Once the eggplants are cool enough to handle, peel off the charred skin and place the flesh in a colander to drain for about 10 minutes. Then, transfer the eggplant flesh to a food processor. Add the tahini, minced garlic, lemon juice, and olive oil. Blend until smooth. Season with salt and pepper to taste. For a creamier texture, you can add an extra tablespoon of tahini.
3. **Serve:** Transfer the baba ganoush to a serving bowl. Drizzle with olive oil and garnish with chopped parsley. Serve with warm or toasted pita bread. For added flavour, sprinkle some paprika or cumin on top before serving.

ESTIMATED NUTRITIONAL INFORMATION PER SERVING:
Calories: approx. 180 kcal | Fat: approx. 10 g | Carbohydrates: approx. 20 g | Fibre: approx. 5 g | Protein: approx. 3 g | Salt: approx. 0.4 g

GRILLED HALLOUMI WITH LEMON AND THYME

Golden grilled halloumi served with a squeeze of lemon and a sprinkle of thyme, a simple yet flavorful appetiser.

Portions: 4 | **Difficulty Level:** Easy | **Preparation Time:** 5 minutes | **Cooking Time:** 10 minutes | **Total Time:** 15 minutes

INGREDIENTS:
- 250 g halloumi cheese, sliced into 1 cm thick pieces
- 2 tablespoons olive oil
- 1 lemon, zest and juice
- 1 tablespoon fresh thyme leaves
- Freshly ground black pepper to taste
- Lemon wedges for serving

INSTRUCTIONS:
1. **Preheat the grill:** Preheat your grill or grill pan to medium-high heat. Ensuring the grill is hot before cooking will help prevent the cheese from sticking and ensure a nice sear.
2. **Prepare the halloumi:** Brush each slice of halloumi lightly with olive oil. Sprinkle the lemon zest and thyme leaves over the cheese, and season with freshly ground black pepper. The lemon zest will add a fresh, citrusy brightness to the salty halloumi.
3. **Grill the halloumi:** Place the halloumi slices on the hot grill. Cook for 3-5 minutes on each side, or until golden brown grill marks appear. Be careful not to overcook, as halloumi can become too firm if left on the heat for too long.
4. **Finish and serve:** Remove the halloumi from the grill and squeeze some fresh lemon juice over the top before serving. Serve immediately with additional lemon wedges on the side. Serving the halloumi hot ensures it retains its deliciously chewy texture.

ESTIMATED NUTRITIONAL INFORMATION PER SERVING:
Calories: approx. 200 kcal | Fat: approx. 16 g | Carbohydrates: approx. 2 g | Fibre: approx. 0 g | Protein: approx. 12 g | Salt: approx. 1.2 g

TZATZIKI WITH CUCUMBER AND DILL

A refreshing yoghourt dip flavoured with cucumber, garlic, and dill, perfect for dipping veggies or pita chips.

Portions: 4 | **Difficulty Level:** Easy | **Preparation Time:** 10 minutes | **Total Time:** 10 minutes (plus chilling)

INGREDIENTS:

- 1 large cucumber, peeled, seeded, and finely grated
- 500 g Greek yoghourt
- 2 cloves garlic, minced
- 2 tablespoons fresh dill, finely chopped
- 1 tablespoon lemon juice
- 1 tablespoon olive oil
- Salt and freshly ground black pepper to taste

INSTRUCTIONS:

1. **Prepare the cucumber:** After grating the cucumber, place it in a colander, sprinkle with a little salt, and let it sit for a few minutes to draw out excess moisture. Squeeze out as much water as possible using your hands or a clean dish towel. This step is crucial to prevent the tzatziki from becoming watery.
2. **Mix the ingredients:** In a medium bowl, combine the strained cucumber, Greek yoghourt, minced garlic, chopped dill, lemon juice, and olive oil. Stir until well blended. Season with salt and freshly ground black pepper to taste. Adjust the garlic and dill according to your preference for a stronger or milder flavour.
3. **Chill and serve:** Cover the bowl and refrigerate for at least 30 minutes to allow the flavours to meld together. Serve chilled, drizzled with a little more olive oil if desired. Tzatziki is perfect as a dip for vegetables, pita bread, or as a refreshing sauce for grilled meats.

ESTIMATED NUTRITIONAL INFORMATION PER SERVING:
Calories: approx. 120 kcal | Fat: approx. 5 g | Carbohydrates: approx. 8 g | Fibre: approx. 1 g | Protein: approx. 9 g | Salt: approx. 0.4 g

FALAFEL WITH TAHINI SAUCE

Crispy falafel balls served with a creamy tahini sauce, ideal for snacking or as part of a mezze platter.

Portions: 4 | **Difficulty Level:** Medium | **Preparation Time:** 20 minutes (plus soaking time) | **Cooking Time:** 10 minutes | **Total Time:** 30 minutes (excluding soaking)

INGREDIENTS:

- 300 g dried chickpeas, soaked overnight and drained
- 1 onion, chopped
- 2 cloves garlic, minced
- 2 tablespoons fresh parsley, chopped
- 2 tablespoons fresh cilantro, chopped
- 1 teaspoon ground cumin
- 1 teaspoon ground coriander
- 1/2 teaspoon cayenne pepper (adjust to taste)
- Salt and freshly ground black pepper to taste
- Vegetable oil for frying

For the Tahini Sauce:
- 100 g tahini
- 2 tablespoons lemon juice
- 1 clove garlic, minced
- Water, as needed
- Salt to taste

INSTRUCTIONS:

1. **Prepare the falafel mixture:** In a food processor, combine the soaked chickpeas, onion, garlic, parsley, cilantro, cumin, coriander, and cayenne pepper. Process until the mixture is finely ground. Season with salt and pepper. Transfer to a bowl and let it rest for 15 minutes to allow the flavours to meld.
2. **Form the falafel:** Shape the mixture into small balls or patties, about the size of a walnut.
3. **Fry the falafel:** Heat about 2 inches of vegetable oil in a deep skillet over medium-high heat. Fry the falafel in batches, turning occasionally, until golden and crispy, about 4-5 minutes. Remove with a slotted spoon and drain on paper towels.
4. **Make the tahini sauce:** In a small bowl, whisk together tahini, lemon juice, minced garlic, and salt. Gradually add water until the sauce reaches your desired consistency.
5. **Serve:** Serve the falafel hot with the tahini sauce drizzled over or on the side for dipping.

ESTIMATED NUTRITIONAL INFORMATION PER SERVING:
Calories: approx. 350 kcal | Fat: approx. 18 g | Carbohydrates: approx. 40 g | Fibre: approx. 9 g | Protein: approx. 13 g | Salt: approx. 0.8 g

SPICED LENTIL PATTIES WITH HARISSA YOGURT

Flavourful lentil patties served with a cooling yoghourt sauce, spiced with harissa for a little kick.

Portions: 4 | **Difficulty Level:** Medium | **Preparation Time:** 20 minutes | **Cooking Time:** 10 minutes | **Total Time:** 30 minutes

INGREDIENTS:

- 200 g cooked green lentils
- 1 small onion, finely chopped
- 2 cloves garlic, minced
- 1 carrot, grated
- 2 tablespoons fresh cilantro, chopped
- 1 teaspoon ground cumin
- 1/2 teaspoon ground coriander
- Salt and freshly ground black pepper to taste
- 1 egg, beaten
- 50 g breadcrumbs
- Olive oil for frying

For the Harissa Yogurt:
- 200 g Greek yoghourt
- 1 tablespoon harissa paste
- 1 tablespoon lemon juice
- Salt to taste

INSTRUCTIONS:

1. **Prepare the lentil mixture:** In a large bowl, mash the cooked lentils until mostly smooth. Mix in the onion, garlic, grated carrot, cilantro, cumin, and coriander. Season with salt and pepper. Add the beaten egg and breadcrumbs and stir until the mixture is well combined and can be shaped into patties.
2. **Form the patties:** Divide the lentil mixture into equal portions and shape into small, round patties. Using damp hands can help prevent the mixture from sticking.
3. **Cook the patties:** Heat a thin layer of olive oil in a frying-pan over medium heat. Fry the patties in batches, about 2–3 minutes per side, until golden brown and crispy.
4. **Prepare the harissa yoghourt:** While the patties are cooking, mix together the Greek yoghourt, harissa paste, and lemon juice in a small bowl. Season with salt to taste.
5. **Serve:** Serve the spiced lentil patties warm with a dollop of harissa yoghourt on top or on the side for dipping. These patties can be served as part of a larger meal with a side salad or roasted vegetables.

ESTIMATED NUTRITIONAL INFORMATION PER SERVING:
Calories: approx. 280 kcal | Fat: approx. 9 g | Carbohydrates: approx. 35 g | Fibre: approx. 8 g | Protein: approx. 14 g | Salt: approx. 0.7 g

CAPRESE SKEWERS WITH BASIL AND BALSAMIC GLAZE

Mini skewers of fresh mozzarella, cherry tomatoes, and basil, drizzled with a sweet balsamic glaze for a burst of flavour in each bite.

Portions: 4 | **Difficulty Level:** Easy | **Preparation Time:** 10 minutes | **Total Time:** 10 minutes

INGREDIENTS:
- 16 cherry tomatoes
- 16 small balls of fresh mozzarella cheese
- 16 fresh basil leaves
- 2 tablespoons olive oil
- Salt and freshly ground black pepper to taste
- Balsamic glaze for drizzling
- 8 wooden skewers

INSTRUCTIONS:
1. **Assemble the skewers:** Thread a cherry tomato, a basil leaf, and a mozzarella ball onto each skewer. Repeat the sequence until each skewer has two sets of each ingredient. Ensure the skewers are assembled just before serving to maintain the freshness and prevent the basil from wilting.
2. **Season:** Drizzle the assembled skewers with olive oil and season with salt and freshly ground black pepper. The olive oil helps enhance the flavours and adds a smooth texture to the skewers.
3. **Serve with balsamic glaze:** Arrange the skewers on a platter and drizzle with balsamic glaze just before serving. The balsamic glaze adds a sweet and tangy finish that complements the creamy mozzarella and fresh tomatoes perfectly.

ESTIMATED NUTRITIONAL INFORMATION PER SERVING:
Calories: approx. 150 kcal | Fat: approx. 12 g | Carbohydrates: approx. 3 g | Fibre: approx. 1 g | Protein: approx. 8 g | Salt: approx. 0.3 g

CHAPTER 3: SALADS & SIDES

Fresh, vibrant salads and side dishes using Mediterranean staples like olive oil, herbs, and legumes, alongside UK seasonal vegetables.

CLASSIC GREEK SALAD WITH LOCAL FETA AND TOMATOES

A refreshing mix of ripe tomatoes, crisp cucumbers, olives, and tangy feta cheese, using local UK produce.

Portions: 4 | **Difficulty Level:** Easy | **Preparation Time:** 10 minutes | **Total Time:** 10 minutes

INGREDIENTS:
- 4 ripe tomatoes, cut into wedges
- 1 cucumber, peeled and sliced
- 1 red onion, thinly sliced
- 200 g local feta cheese, crumbled
- 100 g Kalamata olives
- 2 tablespoons extra virgin olive oil
- 1 tablespoon red wine vinegar
- Salt and freshly ground black pepper to taste
- A handful of fresh oregano or basil leaves

INSTRUCTIONS:
1. **Combine the vegetables:** In a large salad bowl, combine the tomato wedges, cucumber slices, and red onion. Gently toss the vegetables to mix their flavours without breaking them up too much.
2. **Add cheese and olives:** Sprinkle the crumbled feta cheese and Kalamata olives over the vegetables.
3. **Dress the salad:** Drizzle the extra virgin olive oil and red wine vinegar over the salad. Season with salt and freshly ground black pepper to taste. For an authentic Greek flavour, you can add a little dried oregano along with the fresh herbs.
4. **Garnish and serve:** Toss the salad gently to coat everything evenly with the dressing. Garnish with fresh oregano or basil leaves just before serving. This salad is perfect as a standalone light meal or as a refreshing side dish to grilled meats.

ESTIMATED NUTRITIONAL INFORMATION PER SERVING:
Calories: approx. 250 kcal | Fat: approx. 20 g | Carbohydrates: approx. 10 g | Fibre: approx. 3 g | Protein: approx. 8 g | Salt: approx. 1.2 g

WARM LENTIL SALAD WITH ROASTED ROOT VEGETABLES AND TAHINI DRESSING

Earthy lentils combined with roasted root vegetables create a warm, hearty salad, drizzled with a rich tahini dressing.

Portions: 4 | **Difficulty Level:** Easy | **Preparation Time:** 20 minutes | **Cooking Time:** 30 minutes | **Total Time:** 50 minutes

INGREDIENTS:

- 200 g dried green lentils, rinsed and drained
- 300 g mixed root vegetables (such as carrots, parsnips, and beets), peeled and diced
- 2 tablespoons olive oil
- Salt and freshly ground black pepper to taste
- Fresh parsley, chopped for garnish

For the Tahini Dressing:
- 3 tablespoons tahini
- 2 tablespoons lemon juice
- 1 clove garlic, minced
- Water, as needed to thin the dressing
- Salt to taste

INSTRUCTIONS:

1. **Cook the lentils:** In a medium saucepan, cover the lentils with water and bring to a boil. Reduce heat to a simmer and cook for 20-25 minutes, or until tender. Drain any excess water and set aside.
2. **Roast the vegetables:** Preheat your oven to 200°C (400°F). Toss the diced root vegetables with olive oil, salt, and pepper on a baking sheet. Roast in the oven for 20-30 minutes, turning occasionally, until tender and caramelised.
3. **Prepare the tahini dressing:** While the vegetables are roasting, whisk together the tahini, lemon juice, minced garlic, and salt in a small bowl. Gradually add water until the dressing reaches your desired consistency. The dressing should be creamy but pourable.
4. **Assemble the salad:** In a large mixing bowl, combine the warm lentils and roasted vegetables. Drizzle with the tahini dressing and toss gently to coat. Adjust seasoning as needed.
5. **Serve:** Transfer the salad to a serving dish and garnish with chopped parsley. Serve warm. This salad makes a hearty side dish or can be enjoyed as a light main course.

ESTIMATED NUTRITIONAL INFORMATION PER SERVING:
Calories: approx. 320 kcal | Fat: approx. 12 g | Carbohydrates: approx. 40 g | Fibre: approx. 15 g | Protein: approx. 14 g | Salt: approx. 0.3 g

CHARRED BROCCOLI AND CAULIFLOWER WITH GARLIC LEMON DRESSING

Roasted broccoli and cauliflower, finished with a zesty garlic-lemon dressing for a smoky, vibrant side dish.

Portions: 4 | **Difficulty Level:** Easy | **Preparation Time:** 10 minutes | **Cooking Time:** 20 minutes | **Total Time:** 30 minutes

INGREDIENTS:

- 300 g broccoli, cut into florets
- 300 g cauliflower, cut into florets
- 2 tablespoons olive oil
- Salt and freshly ground black pepper to taste

For the Garlic Lemon Dressing:
- 3 tablespoons olive oil
- 1 lemon, juice and zest
- 2 cloves garlic, minced
- Salt and pepper to taste

INSTRUCTIONS:

1. **Preheat the grill:** Preheat your oven's grill or a grill pan on the stove over high heat. Ensure it's very hot before adding the vegetables to achieve a good char.
2. **Prepare the vegetables:** Toss the broccoli and cauliflower florets with 2 tablespoons of olive oil, salt, and pepper. Arrange the florets in a single layer on a baking sheet or grill pan. Make sure not to overcrowd the pan to allow each piece to char nicely.
3. **Grill the vegetables:** Grill the broccoli and cauliflower for 10-15 minutes, turning occasionally, until they are charred at the edges and tender. The high heat will help to caramelise the florets and bring out their natural sweetness.
4. **Make the dressing:** While the vegetables are grilling, whisk together the remaining olive oil, lemon juice, lemon zest, and minced garlic in a small bowl. Season with salt and pepper to taste. Adjust the acidity by adding more lemon juice or olive oil as needed.
5. **Finish and serve:** Once the vegetables are charred and tender, remove them from the grill. Drizzle the garlic lemon dressing over the hot vegetables and toss gently to coat. The heat from the vegetables will mellow the raw garlic slightly, blending the flavours beautifully.
6. **Serve:** Transfer the dressed vegetables to a serving dish and serve immediately, while warm. This dish is perfect as a side for roasted or grilled meats, or can be enjoyed on its own as a light vegetarian option.

ESTIMATED NUTRITIONAL INFORMATION PER SERVING:
Calories: approx. 180 kcal | Fat: approx. 14 g | Carbohydrates: approx. 12 g | Fibre: approx. 4 g | Protein: approx. 4 g | Salt: approx. 0.2 g

BULGUR WHEAT SALAD WITH POMEGRANATE AND FRESH HERBS

A colourful salad combining bulgur wheat, fresh herbs, and juicy pomegranate seeds for a delightful mix of flavours and textures.

Portions: 4 | **Difficulty Level:** Easy | **Preparation Time:** 15 minutes | **Total Time:** 15 minutes

INGREDIENTS:

- 200 g bulgur wheat
- 1 pomegranate, seeds removed
- 1 cucumber, diced
- 2 spring onions, finely sliced
- 1 handful of fresh parsley, chopped
- 1 handful of fresh mint, chopped
- 3 tablespoons olive oil
- Juice of 1 lemon
- Salt and freshly ground black pepper to taste

INSTRUCTIONS:

1. **Prepare the bulgur wheat:** Cook the bulgur wheat according to package instructions, usually by boiling in water for 10-12 minutes or until tender. Drain any excess water and let it cool slightly. Fluff it with a fork to prevent clumping and to help it cool more quickly.
2. **Combine the salad ingredients:** In a large mixing bowl, combine the cooled bulgur wheat, pomegranate seeds, diced cucumber, sliced spring onions, chopped parsley, and mint. The freshness of the herbs and the crunch of the pomegranate seeds will add vibrant flavours and textures to the salad.
3. **Dress the salad:** Whisk together the olive oil and lemon juice in a small bowl. Season with salt and pepper. Pour this dressing over the salad and toss well to ensure everything is evenly coated. Adjust the seasoning according to your taste, adding more lemon juice or olive oil if needed.
4. **Chill and serve:** Let the salad sit for a few minutes to allow the flavours to meld together, or chill in the refrigerator before serving. This resting period helps the bulgur wheat to absorb the dressing and the flavours to develop.
5. **Serve:** This salad can be served as a light lunch or as a side dish with grilled meats or fish. It's particularly good with grilled lamb or chicken.

ESTIMATED NUTRITIONAL INFORMATION PER SERVING:
Calories: approx. 270 kcal | Fat: approx. 10 g | Carbohydrates: approx. 40 g | Fibre: approx. 7 g | Protein: approx. 6 g | Salt: approx. 0.3 g

FENNEL AND ORANGE SALAD WITH OLIVE OIL AND BLACK OLIVES

Crisp fennel slices paired with sweet, juicy orange segments and briny black olives, all drizzled with olive oil for a refreshing salad.

Portions: 4 | **Difficulty Level:** Easy | **Preparation Time:** 10 minutes | **Total Time:** 10 minutes

INGREDIENTS:
- 2 large fennel bulbs, thinly sliced
- 3 oranges, peeled and segments cut out
- 100 g black olives, pitted and halved
- 3 tablespoons extra virgin olive oil
- 1 tablespoon white wine vinegar
- Salt and freshly ground black pepper to taste
- Fresh parsley, chopped for garnish

INSTRUCTIONS:
1. **Prepare the ingredients:** Use a mandoline or sharp knife to thinly slice the fennel bulbs. Segment the oranges by cutting between the membranes to release the segments, catching any juice that drips for the dressing.
2. **Assemble the salad:** In a large salad bowl, combine the sliced fennel, orange segments, and halved black olives. The contrast in flavours and textures between the crisp fennel, sweet oranges, and salty olives creates a vibrant dish.
3. **Dress the salad:** Whisk together the olive oil, white wine vinegar, and any caught orange juice in a small bowl. Season with salt and pepper. Drizzle this dressing over the salad and gently toss to coat all the ingredients. Adjust the seasoning to taste, and add more olive oil or vinegar if needed for balance.
4. **Garnish and serve:** Sprinkle chopped parsley over the salad for a fresh, herbal finish. Serve immediately to enjoy the crispness of the fennel and the freshness of the oranges at their best. This salad pairs beautifully with seafood dishes or can be a refreshing start to any meal.

ESTIMATED NUTRITIONAL INFORMATION PER SERVING:
Calories: approx. 180 kcal | Fat: approx. 11 g | Carbohydrates: approx. 20 g | Fibre: approx. 5 g | Protein: approx. 2 g | Salt: approx. 0.6 g

GRILLED AUBERGINE WITH TAHINI AND PINE NUTS

Smoky grilled aubergine slices drizzled with creamy tahini and sprinkled with toasted pine nuts for a simple yet rich side.

Portions: 4 | **Difficulty Level:** Easy | **Preparation Time:** 10 minutes | **Cooking Time:** 15 minutes | **Total Time:** 25 minutes

INGREDIENTS:

- 2 large aubergines, sliced lengthwise into 1/2 inch thick slices
- 3 tablespoons olive oil
- Salt and freshly ground black pepper to taste
- 2 tablespoons pine nuts, toasted
- Fresh parsley, chopped for garnish

For the Tahini Sauce:
- 3 tablespoons tahini
- 1 lemon, juiced
- 1 garlic clove, minced
- Water, as needed to thin the sauce
- Salt to taste

INSTRUCTIONS:

1. **Prep the aubergines:** Brush the aubergine slices with olive oil and season both sides with salt and pepper. This helps to bring out the natural flavours and assists in grilling.
2. **Grill the aubergine:** Preheat a grill or grill pan over medium-high heat. Grill the aubergine slices for about 7-8 minutes on each side, or until they are tender and have nice grill marks. Turning them occasionally ensures even cooking and perfect char lines.
3. **Make the tahini sauce:** While the aubergines are grilling, whisk together the tahini, lemon juice, minced garlic, and salt in a small bowl. Gradually add water until the sauce reaches a pourable consistency. Adjust the seasoning as needed to balance the nuttiness of the tahini with the acidity of the lemon.
4. **Assemble the dish:** Arrange the grilled aubergine slices on a serving platter. Drizzle with the tahini sauce and sprinkle toasted pine nuts over the top. Garnish with chopped parsley. The pine nuts add a delightful crunch and nutty flavour that compliments the creamy tahini and smoky aubergine.
5. **Serve:** This dish can be served warm or at room temperature, making it versatile for various meal settings. It's perfect as a side dish or can be featured as a main component in a vegetarian feast.

ESTIMATED NUTRITIONAL INFORMATION PER SERVING:
Calories: approx. 250 kcal | Fat: approx. 20 g | Carbohydrates: approx. 18 g | Fibre: approx. 6 g | Protein: approx. 5 g | Salt: approx. 0.4 g

QUINOA TABBOULEH WITH FRESH PARSLEY AND MINT

A light and refreshing salad made with fluffy quinoa, fresh parsley, mint, and lemon juice for a citrusy kick.

Portions: 4 | **Difficulty Level:** Easy | **Preparation Time:** 15 minutes | **Total Time:** 15 minutes (plus time for quinoa to cool)

INGREDIENTS:

- 200 g quinoa, cooked and cooled
- 1 large bunch of fresh parsley, finely chopped
- 1 small bunch of fresh mint, finely chopped
- 2 medium tomatoes, diced
- 1 cucumber, diced
- 1 small red onion, finely chopped
- Juice of 2 lemons
- 3 tablespoons olive oil
- Salt and freshly ground black pepper to taste

INSTRUCTIONS:

1. **Prepare the quinoa:** Cook the quinoa according to package instructions. Allow it to cool completely before using in the salad. Fluff the quinoa with a fork to ensure it's light and airy.
2. **Combine the ingredients:** In a large bowl, mix together the cooked quinoa, chopped parsley, mint, tomatoes, cucumber, and red onion. The herbs should be fresh and vibrant, providing the signature flavour of traditional tabbouleh.
3. **Dress the salad:** Whisk together the lemon juice, olive oil, salt, and pepper in a small bowl. Pour this dressing over the quinoa mixture and toss gently to combine everything evenly. Adjust the lemon juice and olive oil to taste, depending on your preference for acidity and richness.
4. **Chill and serve:** Let the salad sit for at least 30 minutes in the refrigerator before serving to allow the flavours to meld together. This also chills the salad, which enhances its refreshing quality. Tabbouleh is best served cold and can be kept in the refrigerator for a couple of days.
5. **Serve:** This salad is perfect as a light lunch or as a side dish to grilled meats. It's particularly good with grilled chicken or fish. Garnish with additional fresh herbs just before serving to enhance the presentation.

ESTIMATED NUTRITIONAL INFORMATION PER SERVING:

Calories: approx. 240 kcal | Fat: approx. 10 g | Carbohydrates: approx. 33 g | Fibre: approx. 5 g | Protein: approx. 6 g | Salt: approx. 0.2 g

MEDITERRANEAN POTATO SALAD WITH OLIVES AND CAPERS

A twist on classic potato salad, this version uses a light olive oil dressing and is packed with olives, capers, and fresh herbs.

Portions: 4 | **Difficulty Level:** Easy | **Preparation Time:** 15 minutes | **Cooking Time:** 20 minutes | **Total Time:** 35 minutes

INGREDIENTS:

- 500 g new potatoes, halved or quartered depending on size
- 100 g Kalamata olives, pitted and halved
- 2 tablespoons capers, rinsed
- 1 small red onion, thinly sliced
- 1 handful of fresh parsley, chopped
- 2 tablespoons extra virgin olive oil
- Juice of 1 lemon
- 1 clove garlic, minced
- Salt and freshly ground black pepper to taste

INSTRUCTIONS:

1. **Cook the potatoes:** Place the potatoes in a large pot of salted water. Bring to a boil and cook until tender but still firm, about 15-20 minutes. Drain and let them cool slightly.
2. **Prepare the dressing:** While the potatoes are cooking, whisk together the olive oil, lemon juice, minced garlic, salt, and pepper in a small bowl. This simple Mediterranean-style dressing will bring bright and tangy flavours to the salad.
3. **Combine the ingredients:** In a large bowl, combine the warm potatoes, olives, capers, red onion, and chopped parsley. Pour the dressing over the salad and toss gently to coat. The warm potatoes will absorb the flavours of the dressing more effectively.
4. **Chill and serve:** Allow the salad to sit for at least 10 minutes before serving to let the flavours meld together. This salad can be served warm, at room temperature, or chilled. For best results, let the salad chill for a couple of hours in the refrigerator.
5. **Serve:** This potato salad is perfect as a side dish for grilled meats or as part of a picnic spread. The bold flavours of the olives and capers make it a standout dish that pairs well with milder main courses.

ESTIMATED NUTRITIONAL INFORMATION PER SERVING:
Calories: approx. 250 kcal | Fat: approx. 10 g | Carbohydrates: approx. 35 g | Fibre: approx. 4 g | Protein: approx. 4 g | Salt: approx. 0.8 g

ROASTED CARROTS WITH HONEY AND THYME

Tender roasted carrots with a sweet honey glaze and the earthy notes of fresh thyme, perfect for pairing with any main dish.

Portions: 4 | **Difficulty Level:** Easy | **Preparation Time:** 10 minutes | **Cooking Time:** 25 minutes | **Total Time:** 35 minutes

INGREDIENTS:
- 500 g carrots, peeled and sliced lengthwise
- 2 tablespoons olive oil
- 2 tablespoons honey
- 1 tablespoon fresh thyme leaves
- Salt and freshly ground black pepper to taste

INSTRUCTIONS:
1. **Preheat the oven:** Set your oven to 200°C (400°F). This high temperature is perfect for roasting, giving the carrots a nicely caramelised exterior.
2. **Prepare the carrots:** In a large bowl, toss the carrots with olive oil, honey, thyme, salt, and pepper until evenly coated. The honey will not only add sweetness but also help to caramelise the carrots during roasting.
3. **Roast the carrots:** Spread the carrots in a single layer on a baking sheet. Roast in the preheated oven for 25 minutes, turning once halfway through, until the carrots are tender and caramelised. Ensure the carrots have enough space on the baking sheet to roast evenly without steaming.
4. **Serve:** Remove from the oven and adjust seasoning with additional salt and pepper if needed. Serve warm as a side dish. These roasted carrots are a versatile side that pairs well with both meat and vegetarian main courses, adding a sweet and earthy element to your meal.

ESTIMATED NUTRITIONAL INFORMATION PER SERVING:
Calories: approx. 160 kcal | Fat: approx. 7 g | Carbohydrates: approx. 24 g | Fibre: approx. 3 g | Protein: approx. 1 g | Salt: approx. 0.3 g

SPINACH AND ORZO SALAD WITH FETA AND LEMON

A light and zesty salad made with orzo pasta, fresh spinach, and tangy feta, tossed with a lemon vinaigrette.

Portions: 4 | **Difficulty Level:** Easy | **Preparation Time:** 10 minutes | **Cooking Time:** 10 minutes | **Total Time:** 20 minutes

INGREDIENTS:

- 200 g orzo pasta
- 200 g fresh spinach, roughly chopped
- 100 g feta cheese, crumbled
- 1 red onion, thinly sliced
- 2 tablespoons olive oil
- Juice and zest of 1 lemon
- Salt and freshly ground black pepper to taste
- Fresh basil leaves, for garnish

INSTRUCTIONS:

1. **Cook the orzo:** Bring a large pot of salted water to a boil. Add the orzo and cook according to package instructions, usually 8-10 minutes, until al dente. Drain and rinse under cold water to cool. Set aside. Rinsing the orzo helps to stop the cooking process and prevents it from sticking together.
2. **Prepare the salad components:** While the orzo is cooking, prepare the rest of the salad. In a large mixing bowl, combine the cooled orzo, chopped spinach, crumbled feta, and thinly sliced red onion.
3. **Make the dressing:** In a small bowl, whisk together the olive oil, lemon juice, lemon zest, salt, and pepper. Adjust the lemon juice and olive oil ratio based on your taste preference for acidity and richness.
4. **Combine and chill:** Pour the dressing over the salad ingredients and toss gently to combine everything evenly. Let the salad sit for a few minutes to allow the flavours to meld together, or chill in the refrigerator for about 10 minutes before serving. This chilling time helps the spinach to slightly wilt and the flavours to intensify.
5. **Garnish and serve:** Before serving, garnish with fresh basil leaves for an additional burst of flavour and colour. This salad can be served as a light main course or as a refreshing side dish alongside grilled meats or seafood.

ESTIMATED NUTRITIONAL INFORMATION PER SERVING:
Calories: approx. 280 kcal | Fat: approx. 10 g | Carbohydrates: approx. 36 g | Fibre: approx. 3 g | Protein: approx. 12 g | Salt: approx. 0.5 g

CHAPTER 4: MAIN COURSES - VEGETARIAN

Plant-based Mediterranean mains, from hearty stews to vibrant vegetable dishes, incorporating local grains and vegetables.

AUBERGINE PARMIGIANA WITH A FRESH TOMATO-BASIL SAUCE

Layered slices of roasted aubergine, baked with a homemade tomato-basil sauce, and topped with melted cheese.

Portions: 4 | **Difficulty Level:** Medium | **Preparation Time:** 20 minutes | **Cooking Time:** 40 minutes | **Total Time:** 1 hour

INGREDIENTS:

- 3 medium aubergines, sliced into 1/2 inch thick rounds
- Salt, to draw out moisture from the aubergines
- Olive oil, for frying
- 400 g canned crushed tomatoes
- 2 cloves garlic, minced
- A handful of fresh basil, chopped
- 200 g mozzarella cheese, sliced
- 100 g Parmesan cheese, grated
- Salt and freshly ground black pepper to taste

INSTRUCTIONS:

1. **Prepare the aubergines:** Sprinkle the aubergine slices with salt and set them aside in a colander for about 30 minutes to draw out moisture. Rinse the slices under cold water, and pat them dry with paper towels.
2. **Fry the aubergines:** Heat a generous amount of olive oil in a frying pan over medium heat. Fry the aubergine slices in batches until golden brown on both sides. Transfer to a paper towel-lined plate to drain.
3. **Make the tomato-basil sauce:** In a saucepan, sauté the minced garlic in a little olive oil until fragrant. Add the crushed tomatoes and simmer for 10 minutes. Stir in the chopped basil and season with salt and pepper to taste.
4. **Assemble the dish:** Preheat your oven to 180°C (350°F). In a baking dish, layer the fried aubergine slices with the tomato-basil sauce, slices of mozzarella, and a sprinkle of Parmesan cheese. Repeat the layers until all ingredients are used, finishing with a layer of cheese on top.
5. **Bake:** Place the dish in the oven and bake for 30 minutes, or until the cheese is bubbling and golden brown.
6. **Serve:** Let the parmigiana rest for a few minutes before serving. This dish pairs well with a fresh salad or crusty bread.

ESTIMATED NUTRITIONAL INFORMATION PER SERVING:
Calories: approx. 400 kcal | Fat: approx. 25 g | Carbohydrates: approx. 30 g | Fibre: approx. 8 g | Protein: approx. 20 g | Salt: approx. 1.2 g

STUFFED PEPPERS WITH QUINOA AND SEASONAL GREENS

Colourful bell peppers filled with a flavorful mix of quinoa, spinach, and fresh herbs, baked until tender.

Portions: 4 | **Difficulty Level:** Easy | **Preparation Time:** 20 minutes | **Cooking Time:** 25 minutes | **Total Time:** 45 minutes

INGREDIENTS:

- 4 large bell peppers, tops cut off and seeds removed
- 200 g quinoa, rinsed
- 400 ml vegetable broth
- 1 small onion, finely chopped
- 2 cloves garlic, minced
- 200 g spinach, washed and roughly chopped
- 100 g feta cheese, crumbled
- A handful of fresh herbs (such as parsley and basil), chopped
- 2 tablespoons olive oil
- Salt and freshly ground black pepper to taste

INSTRUCTIONS:

1. **Cook the quinoa:** In a saucepan, bring the vegetable broth to a boil. Add the quinoa, reduce heat to low, cover, and simmer for 15 minutes or until all the liquid is absorbed. Remove from heat and let sit, covered, for 5 minutes. Fluff with a fork.
2. **Prepare the filling:** While the quinoa cooks, heat the olive oil in a skillet over medium heat. Sauté the onion and garlic until translucent. Add the chopped spinach and cook until just wilted. Remove from heat and stir in the cooked quinoa, crumbled feta, and chopped herbs. Season with salt and pepper.
3. **Stuff the peppers:** Preheat your oven to 190°C (375°F). Spoon the quinoa and greens mixture into the hollowed-out bell peppers. Place the stuffed peppers upright in a baking dish.
4. **Bake:** Cover the dish with foil and bake in the preheated oven for about 20-25 minutes, until the peppers are tender and the filling is heated through.
5. **Serve:** Serve the stuffed peppers hot, with extra herbs or a drizzle of olive oil if desired. These are great on their own or with a side salad for a complete meal.

ESTIMATED NUTRITIONAL INFORMATION PER SERVING:

Calories: approx. 290 kcal | Fat: approx. 10 g | Carbohydrates: approx. 40 g | Fibre: approx. 6 g | Protein: approx. 12 g | Salt: approx. 0.8 g

CHICKPEA AND SPINACH STEW WITH SPICES

A hearty and warming stew made with chickpeas, fresh spinach, and a blend of Mediterranean spices.

Portions: 4 | **Difficulty Level:** Easy | **Preparation Time:** 10 minutes | **Cooking Time:** 20 minutes | **Total Time:** 30 minutes

INGREDIENTS:

- 400 g canned chickpeas, drained and rinsed
- 300 g fresh spinach, washed and roughly chopped
- 1 large onion, finely chopped
- 2 cloves garlic, minced
- 1 teaspoon ground cumin
- 1 teaspoon ground coriander
- 1/2 teaspoon smoked paprika
- 1/4 teaspoon cayenne pepper (adjust to taste)
- 400 ml vegetable broth
- 2 tablespoons olive oil
- Salt and freshly ground black pepper to taste
- Fresh cilantro or parsley for garnish

INSTRUCTIONS:

1. **Sauté the onions and spices:** Heat the olive oil in a large pot over medium heat. Add the chopped onion and garlic, sautéing until the onions are translucent. Stir in the cumin, coriander, paprika, and cayenne pepper, cooking for another minute until fragrant.
2. **Add chickpeas and broth:** Add the chickpeas to the pot, stirring to coat them in the spices. Pour in the vegetable broth and bring the mixture to a simmer. Let it cook for about 10 minutes, allowing the flavours to meld together.
3. **Add the spinach:** Stir in the fresh spinach and cook until it wilts into the stew, about 5 minutes. Adjust the seasoning with salt and black pepper.
4. **Garnish and serve:** Remove the stew from heat. Garnish with chopped cilantro or parsley before serving. This hearty stew is perfect served with crusty bread or over a bed of rice for a complete meal.

ESTIMATED NUTRITIONAL INFORMATION PER SERVING:
Calories: approx. 240 kcal | Fat: approx. 8 g | Carbohydrates: approx. 30 g | Fibre: approx. 8 g | Protein: approx. 10 g | Salt: approx. 1.2 g

MUSHROOM RISOTTO WITH FRESH HERBS

Creamy risotto made with arborio rice, wild mushrooms, and fresh herbs, a rich and comforting vegetarian dish.

Portions: 4 | **Difficulty Level:** Medium | **Preparation Time:** 10 minutes | **Cooking Time:** 30 minutes | **Total Time:** 40 minutes

INGREDIENTS:

- 300 g arborio rice
- 200 g mixed mushrooms (such as cremini, shiitake, or button), sliced
- 1 small onion, finely chopped
- 2 cloves garlic, minced
- 1 litre vegetable broth, kept warm
- 100 ml white wine (optional)
- 2 tablespoons olive oil
- 2 tablespoons butter
- 50 g Parmesan cheese, grated
- A handful of fresh parsley, finely chopped
- A handful of fresh thyme leaves
- Salt and freshly ground black pepper to taste

INSTRUCTIONS:

1. **Sauté the mushrooms:** In a large skillet, heat 1 tablespoon of olive oil over medium heat. Add the sliced mushrooms and cook until they release their moisture and become golden brown, about 5-7 minutes. Set aside.
2. **Cook the onions and garlic:** In the same pan, heat the remaining olive oil and 1 tablespoon of butter over medium heat. Add the chopped onion and garlic, cooking until softened, about 3 minutes.
3. **Toast the rice:** Add the arborio rice to the pan and stir to coat the grains in the oil. Cook for 2-3 minutes until the rice is lightly toasted.
4. **Add the wine and broth:** Pour in the white wine (if using) and stir until mostly absorbed. Begin adding the warm vegetable broth one ladle at a time, stirring constantly. Allow each addition of broth to be absorbed before adding the next. Continue this process until the rice is tender and creamy, about 20-25 minutes.
5. **Finish the risotto:** Stir in the sautéed mushrooms, remaining butter, Parmesan cheese, and fresh herbs. Season with salt and black pepper to taste. For an extra rich texture, you can stir in a little more butter or a drizzle of olive oil at the end.
6. **Serve:** Garnish with additional fresh parsley and thyme before serving. This creamy risotto pairs well with a green salad or roasted vegetables.

ESTIMATED NUTRITIONAL INFORMATION PER SERVING:
Calories: approx. 400 kcal | Fat: approx. 18 g | Carbohydrates: approx. 50 g | Fibre: approx. 3 g | Protein: approx. 12 g | Salt: approx. 1.0 g

VEGETARIAN MOUSSAKA WITH LENTILS AND AUBERGINE

A plant-based version of the classic Greek dish, made with layers of aubergine and a savoury lentil filling, topped with béchamel sauce.

Portions: 4 | **Difficulty Level:** Medium | **Preparation Time:** 30 minutes | **Cooking Time:** 45 minutes | **Total Time:** 1 hour 15 minutes

INGREDIENTS:

- 2 large aubergines, sliced into 1/2 inch thick rounds
- 200 g dried green or brown lentils, rinsed
- 1 onion, finely chopped
- 2 cloves garlic, minced
- 400 g canned crushed tomatoes
- 1 teaspoon ground cinnamon
- 1 teaspoon ground cumin
- 1 tablespoon olive oil
- Salt and freshly ground black pepper to taste

For the Béchamel Sauce:

- 50 g butter
- 50 g all-purpose flour
- 500 ml milk
- 50 g Parmesan cheese, grated
- A pinch of nutmeg

INSTRUCTIONS:

1. **Prepare the aubergines:** Preheat your oven to 200°C (400°F). Arrange the aubergine slices on a baking sheet, drizzle with olive oil, and season with salt and pepper. Roast for 20 minutes, turning halfway through, until golden brown and tender. Set aside.
2. **Cook the lentils:** While the aubergines are roasting, cook the lentils in a pot of boiling water for 20-25 minutes or until tender. Drain and set aside.
3. **Make the lentil filling:** In a large pan, heat 1 tablespoon of olive oil over medium heat. Add the chopped onion and garlic, sautéing until softened. Stir in the ground cinnamon and cumin, cooking for another minute. Add the crushed tomatoes and cooked lentils, season with salt and pepper, and simmer for 10 minutes until the mixture thickens slightly. Remove from heat.
4. **Prepare the béchamel sauce:** In a saucepan, melt the butter over medium heat. Stir in the flour and cook for 1-2 minutes, stirring constantly, to form a roux. Gradually whisk in the milk and cook until the sauce thickens. Remove from heat and stir in the grated Parmesan and a pinch of nutmeg.
5. **Assemble the moussaka:** In a greased baking dish, layer half of the roasted aubergines on the bottom. Spread the lentil filling evenly on top, then layer the remaining aubergines. Pour the béchamel sauce over the top, spreading it out evenly.
6. **Bake:** Reduce the oven temperature to 180°C (350°F). Bake the moussaka for 30 minutes, or until the top is golden and bubbling. Let it cool for 10 minutes before serving.
7. **Serve:** Garnish with fresh herbs, such as parsley, if desired. This vegetarian moussaka is hearty and comforting, perfect for a main course.

ESTIMATED NUTRITIONAL INFORMATION PER SERVING:
Calories: approx. 450 kcal | Fat: approx. 20 g | Carbohydrates: approx. 50 g | Fibre: approx. 12 g | Protein: approx. 18 g | Salt: approx. 1.2 g

FENNEL AND POTATO GRATIN WITH PARMESAN

Thinly sliced fennel and potatoes layered with cream and Parmesan, baked until golden and bubbling.

Portions: 4 | **Difficulty Level:** Medium | **Preparation Time:** 15 minutes | **Cooking Time:** 1 hour | **Total Time:** 1 hour 15 minutes

INGREDIENTS:

- 2 large fennel bulbs, thinly sliced
- 4 medium potatoes, thinly sliced
- 200 ml double cream
- 200 ml milk
- 100 g Parmesan cheese, grated
- 2 cloves garlic, minced
- 1 tablespoon fresh thyme leaves
- 1 tablespoon olive oil
- Salt and freshly ground black pepper to taste

INSTRUCTIONS:

1. **Preheat the oven:** Preheat your oven to 180°C (350°F). Grease a baking dish with olive oil.
2. **Prepare the gratin layers:** In the greased baking dish, layer half of the sliced potatoes on the bottom. Season with salt and pepper. Add a layer of sliced fennel on top, followed by the remaining potatoes. Sprinkle the minced garlic and fresh thyme over the top layer.
3. **Make the cream mixture:** In a saucepan, combine the double cream and milk. Heat over medium heat until warm but not boiling. Season with salt and pepper. Pour the cream mixture evenly over the fennel and potatoes.
4. **Add the Parmesan:** Sprinkle the grated Parmesan cheese evenly over the top of the gratin.
5. **Bake the gratin:** Cover the baking dish with foil and bake in the preheated oven for 40 minutes. Remove the foil and continue baking for an additional 15-20 minutes, or until the top is golden and the potatoes are tender when pierced with a fork.
6. **Serve:** Let the gratin rest for 5-10 minutes before serving. This dish is a perfect side or main course, paired with a fresh green salad or roasted vegetables.

ESTIMATED NUTRITIONAL INFORMATION PER SERVING:
Calories: approx. 400 kcal | Fat: approx. 25 g | Carbohydrates: approx. 35 g | Fibre: approx. 4 g | Protein: approx. 10 g | Salt: approx. 0.8 g

MEDITERRANEAN VEGETABLE AND COUSCOUS TAGINE

A fragrant and hearty vegetable tagine, served over fluffy couscous with a mix of spices and herbs.

Portions: 4 | **Difficulty Level:** Medium | **Preparation Time:** 15 minutes | **Cooking Time:** 30 minutes | **Total Time:** 45 minutes

INGREDIENTS:

- 1 large courgette, diced
- 1 aubergine, diced
- 1 red bell pepper, diced
- 1 carrot, sliced
- 1 onion, chopped
- 2 cloves garlic, minced
- 200 g couscous
- 400 ml vegetable broth
- 1 can (400 g) chopped tomatoes
- 1 tablespoon olive oil
- 1 teaspoon ground cumin
- 1 teaspoon ground coriander
- 1/2 teaspoon ground cinnamon
- 1/2 teaspoon smoked paprika
- A handful of fresh parsley, chopped
- Salt and freshly ground black pepper to taste
- A handful of toasted almonds for garnish (optional)

INSTRUCTIONS:

1. **Prepare the vegetables:** Heat the olive oil in a large pot or tagine over medium heat. Add the chopped onion and garlic, sautéing until softened, about 5 minutes. Stir in the cumin, coriander, cinnamon, and paprika, and cook for another minute until fragrant.
2. **Cook the vegetables:** Add the diced courgette, aubergine, bell pepper, and carrot to the pot. Stir to coat the vegetables in the spices, then add the chopped tomatoes. Season with salt and pepper. Cover the pot and let the vegetables simmer for 20-25 minutes, stirring occasionally, until they are tender.
3. **Prepare the couscous:** While the vegetables are cooking, bring the vegetable broth to a boil in a separate pot. Remove from heat, add the couscous, and cover. Let the couscous sit for 5 minutes, then fluff with a fork.
4. **Combine and serve:** Once the vegetables are tender, stir in the chopped parsley. Serve the vegetable tagine over the couscous and garnish with toasted almonds if desired. For a richer flavour, drizzle a little extra virgin olive oil over the dish before serving.

ESTIMATED NUTRITIONAL INFORMATION PER SERVING:
Calories: approx. 350 kcal | Fat: approx. 8 g | Carbohydrates: approx. 60 g | Fibre: approx. 10 g | Protein: approx. 9 g | Salt: approx. 0.8 g

SPAGHETTI WITH FRESH TOMATOES, BASIL, AND OLIVE OIL

A simple yet flavorful pasta dish made with ripe tomatoes, fresh basil, and a generous drizzle of olive oil.

Portions: 4 | **Difficulty Level:** Easy | **Preparation Time:** 10 minutes | **Cooking Time:** 15 minutes | **Total Time:** 25 minutes

INGREDIENTS:

- 400 g spaghetti
- 500 g ripe cherry tomatoes, halved
- 2 cloves garlic, minced
- A handful of fresh basil leaves, torn
- 4 tablespoons extra virgin olive oil
- Salt and freshly ground black pepper to taste
- Parmesan cheese, grated (optional)

INSTRUCTIONS:

1. **Cook the spaghetti:** Bring a large pot of salted water to a boil. Add the spaghetti and cook according to the package instructions until al dente. Drain, reserving 1/2 cup of the pasta water, and set aside.
2. **Prepare the sauce:** While the spaghetti is cooking, heat 2 tablespoons of olive oil in a large skillet over medium heat. Add the minced garlic and sauté for 1-2 minutes until fragrant, but not browned. Add the halved cherry tomatoes, season with salt and pepper, and cook for 5-7 minutes until the tomatoes soften and release their juices.
3. **Combine with spaghetti:** Add the cooked spaghetti to the skillet with the tomato sauce, tossing everything together. If the sauce is too thick, stir in a little of the reserved pasta water to loosen it. Remove from heat and stir in the torn basil leaves and remaining olive oil.
4. **Serve:** Divide the spaghetti between plates and top with grated Parmesan cheese, if desired. Serve immediately with extra basil for garnish. This simple dish is perfect for a light meal or can be paired with a green salad or garlic bread for a more complete dinner.

ESTIMATED NUTRITIONAL INFORMATION PER SERVING:
Calories: approx. 450 kcal | Fat: approx. 18 g | Carbohydrates: approx. 60 g | Fibre: approx. 4 g | Protein: approx. 12 g | Salt: approx. 0.6 g

SPINACH AND RICOTTA STUFFED CANNELLONI

Tender cannelloni tubes filled with a creamy spinach and ricotta mixture, baked in a rich tomato sauce.

Portions: 4 | **Difficulty Level:** Medium | **Preparation Time:** 20 minutes | **Cooking Time:** 35 minutes | **Total Time:** 55 minutes

INGREDIENTS:

- 12 cannelloni tubes (uncooked)
- 300 g fresh spinach, washed and roughly chopped
- 250 g ricotta cheese
- 50 g Parmesan cheese, grated
- 1 egg, beaten
- 2 cloves garlic, minced
- 500 ml tomato passata
- 1 teaspoon dried oregano
- 1 tablespoon olive oil
- Salt and freshly ground black pepper to taste
- Fresh basil for garnish (optional)

INSTRUCTIONS:

1. **Preheat the oven:** Preheat your oven to 180°C (350°F).
2. **Prepare the spinach filling:** Heat a tablespoon of olive oil in a pan over medium heat. Add the minced garlic and sauté until fragrant, about 1 minute. Add the chopped spinach and cook until wilted, about 3-4 minutes. Remove from heat, drain any excess moisture, and let it cool slightly.
3. **Mix the filling:** In a large bowl, combine the cooked spinach, ricotta cheese, grated Parmesan, and the beaten egg. Season with salt and freshly ground black pepper. Mix until well combined.
4. **Fill the cannelloni:** Using a small spoon or piping bag, fill the uncooked cannelloni tubes with the spinach and ricotta mixture. Place them in a greased baking dish in a single layer.
5. **Prepare the sauce:** In a bowl, mix the tomato passata with the dried oregano and season with salt and pepper. Pour the sauce over the filled cannelloni, making sure they are completely covered with sauce.
6. **Bake:** Cover the dish with foil and bake for 25 minutes. Remove the foil, sprinkle with additional Parmesan (optional), and bake for another 10 minutes, or until the cannelloni are cooked through and the sauce is bubbling.
7. **Serve:** Garnish with fresh basil leaves, if desired, and serve hot. This dish pairs well with a crisp green salad or garlic bread.

ESTIMATED NUTRITIONAL INFORMATION PER SERVING:
Calories: approx. 400 kcal | Fat: approx. 18 g | Carbohydrates: approx. 45 g | Fibre: approx. 4 g | Protein: approx. 18 g | Salt: approx. 1.0 g

ZUCCHINI NOODLES WITH PESTO AND CHERRY TOMATOES

A light and fresh dish made with spiralized zucchini, tossed in a basil pesto and topped with juicy cherry tomatoes.

Portions: 4 | **Difficulty Level:** Easy | **Preparation Time:** 15 minutes | **Cooking Time:** 5 minutes | **Total Time:** 20 minutes

INGREDIENTS:

- 4 medium zucchinis, spiralized into noodles
- 200 g cherry tomatoes, halved
- 100 g fresh basil pesto (homemade or store-bought)
- 2 tablespoons olive oil
- Salt and freshly ground black pepper to taste
- Fresh basil leaves for garnish
- Parmesan cheese, grated (optional)

INSTRUCTIONS:

1. **Prepare the zucchini noodles:** Using a spiralizer, create noodles from the zucchinis. If you don't have a spiralizer, you can use a vegetable peeler to make thin ribbons. Set aside.
2. **Sauté the tomatoes:** In a large pan, heat the olive oil over medium heat. Add the halved cherry tomatoes and sauté for 3-4 minutes until they soften slightly and release some of their juices. Season with salt and pepper.
3. **Add the zucchini noodles:** Add the zucchini noodles to the pan with the tomatoes. Cook for 1-2 minutes, tossing gently, just until the noodles are slightly tender but still have a bit of crunch. Be careful not to overcook the zucchini noodles, as they can become too soft and watery.
4. **Add the pesto:** Remove the pan from the heat and stir in the fresh pesto, tossing the zucchini noodles and tomatoes until they are evenly coated.
5. **Serve:** Divide the zucchini noodles between plates and garnish with fresh basil leaves. Add grated Parmesan cheese if desired. This dish is light and refreshing, perfect for a quick lunch or dinner.

ESTIMATED NUTRITIONAL INFORMATION PER SERVING:
Calories: approx. 220 kcal | Fat: approx. 18 g | Carbohydrates: approx. 10 g | Fibre: approx. 3 g | Protein: approx. 5 g | Salt: approx. 0.5 g

STUFFED ZUCCHINI WITH QUINOA AND FETA

A hearty and nutritious vegetarian dish featuring zucchini stuffed with a flavorful mixture of quinoa, feta, and fresh herbs. Perfect for a light but satisfying main course.

Portions: 4 | **Difficulty Level:** Medium | **Preparation Time:** 15 minutes | **Cooking Time:** 25 minutes | **Total Time:** 40 minutes

INGREDIENTS:

- 4 medium zucchini, halved lengthwise
- 150 g quinoa, rinsed
- 300 ml vegetable broth
- 100 g feta cheese, crumbled
- 2 tablespoons olive oil
- 1 small onion, finely chopped
- 2 cloves garlic, minced
- 1 tablespoon fresh parsley, chopped
- 1 tablespoon fresh mint, chopped
- 1 tablespoon fresh dill, chopped
- Salt and freshly ground black pepper to taste
- 1 tablespoon lemon juice

INSTRUCTIONS:

1. **Cook the quinoa:** In a saucepan, bring the vegetable broth to a boil. Add the quinoa, reduce the heat, and simmer for 15 minutes, or until the quinoa is tender and the broth is absorbed. Fluff with a fork and set aside.
2. **Prepare the zucchini:** Preheat the oven to 180°C (350°F). Scoop out the flesh from the halved zucchini, leaving about a 1 cm border. Chop the zucchini flesh and set it aside. Brush the zucchini halves with olive oil, place them on a baking tray, and bake for 10 minutes.
3. **Sauté the vegetables:** In a skillet, heat the remaining olive oil over medium heat. Add the onion, garlic, and chopped zucchini flesh. Sauté for 5-6 minutes until softened.
4. **Combine the filling:** In a bowl, mix the cooked quinoa, sautéed vegetables, crumbled feta, parsley, mint, dill, and lemon juice. Season with salt and freshly ground black pepper to taste.
5. **Stuff the zucchini:** Remove the zucchini halves from the oven and fill each one with the quinoa mixture. Return to the oven and bake for another 10 minutes, until the filling is heated through and the zucchini is tender.
6. **Serve:** Garnish the stuffed zucchini with additional herbs and a drizzle of olive oil. This dish pairs beautifully with a side salad or some crusty bread.

ESTIMATED NUTRITIONAL INFORMATION PER SERVING:

Calories: approx. 250 kcal | Fat: approx. 12 g | Carbohydrates: approx. 25 g | Protein: approx. 10 g | Salt: approx. 0.8 g

AUBERGINE INVOLTINI WITH RICOTTA AND SPINACH

Tender aubergine slices rolled up with a creamy ricotta and spinach filling, baked in a rich tomato sauce. A hearty and delicious vegetarian main course that's perfect for any Mediterranean-inspired meal.

Portions: 4 | **Difficulty Level:** Medium | **Preparation Time:** 20 minutes | **Cooking Time:** 40 minutes | **Total Time:** 1 hour

INGREDIENTS:

- 2 large aubergines, sliced lengthwise into 1 cm thick strips
- 250 g ricotta cheese
- 150 g fresh spinach, sautéed and drained
- 1 egg, beaten
- 2 cloves garlic, minced
- 2 tablespoons olive oil
- 500 ml tomato sauce
- 50 g Parmesan cheese, grated
- 1 tablespoon fresh basil, chopped
- 1 tablespoon fresh parsley, chopped
- Salt and freshly ground black pepper to taste

INSTRUCTIONS:

1. **Prepare the aubergine:** Preheat the oven to 180°C (350°F). Brush the aubergine slices with olive oil and season with salt and pepper. Lay them on a baking tray and roast for 15 minutes, or until softened and golden. Remove from the oven and let cool slightly.
2. **Make the filling:** In a bowl, combine the ricotta, sautéed spinach, beaten egg, minced garlic, Parmesan cheese, basil, parsley, and a pinch of salt and pepper. Mix until well combined.
3. **Assemble the involtini:** Spoon a tablespoon of the ricotta mixture onto the end of each aubergine slice, then roll it up tightly. Repeat with the remaining aubergine slices.
4. **Prepare the baking dish:** Spread a thin layer of tomato sauce on the bottom of a baking dish. Place the aubergine involtini seam-side down in the dish. Pour the remaining tomato sauce over the top, ensuring the rolls are evenly coated.
5. **Bake the dish:** Sprinkle the top with additional Parmesan cheese and bake in the preheated oven for 25–30 minutes, or until the sauce is bubbling, and the cheese is golden.
6. **Serve:** Garnish the aubergine involtini with fresh basil leaves and serve hot. This dish pairs wonderfully with a fresh salad or garlic bread.

ESTIMATED NUTRITIONAL INFORMATION PER SERVING:
Calories: approx. 300 kcal | Fat: approx. 18 g | Carbohydrates: approx. 20 g | Protein: approx. 12 g | Salt: approx. 1.0 g

STUFFED BELL PEPPERS WITH COUSCOUS AND FETA

Colorful bell peppers stuffed with a flavorful couscous mixture, combined with feta cheese, fresh herbs, and spices. A delicious and satisfying vegetarian main course, perfect for any occasion.

Portions: 4 | **Difficulty Level:** Easy | **Preparation Time:** 20 minutes | **Cooking Time:** 30 minutes | **Total Time:** 50 minutes

INGREDIENTS:

- 4 large bell peppers, tops cut off and seeds removed
- 150 g couscous
- 250 ml vegetable broth
- 100 g feta cheese, crumbled
- 1 small onion, finely chopped
- 2 cloves garlic, minced
- 2 tablespoons olive oil
- 1 tablespoon tomato paste
- 1 teaspoon ground cumin
- 1 tablespoon fresh parsley, chopped
- 1 tablespoon fresh mint, chopped
- Salt and freshly ground black pepper to taste
- Lemon wedges for serving

INSTRUCTIONS:

1. **Cook the couscous:** In a saucepan, bring the vegetable broth to a boil. Stir in the couscous, cover, and remove from heat. Let it sit for 5 minutes, then fluff with a fork and set aside.
2. **Sauté the onions and garlic:** In a skillet, heat the olive oil over medium heat. Add the chopped onion and garlic, and sauté for 3-4 minutes until softened. Stir in the tomato paste, cumin, and a pinch of salt and pepper. Cook for another minute.
3. **Mix the stuffing:** In a large bowl, combine the cooked couscous, sautéed onion and garlic mixture, crumbled feta, parsley, and mint. Stir well to combine, and adjust seasoning if necessary.
4. **Prepare the bell peppers:** Preheat the oven to 180°C (350°F). Place the bell peppers upright in a baking dish. Spoon the couscous mixture into each pepper, filling them to the top.
5. **Bake the peppers:** Cover the dish with foil and bake for 25-30 minutes, or until the peppers are tender. Remove the foil in the last 10 minutes of baking to allow the tops to become slightly golden.
6. **Serve:** Serve the stuffed bell peppers with a drizzle of olive oil and lemon wedges on the side. These stuffed peppers make a delicious and colorful vegetarian main course.

ESTIMATED NUTRITIONAL INFORMATION PER SERVING:
Calories: approx. 280 kcal | Fat: approx. 14 g | Carbohydrates: approx. 28 g | Protein: approx. 8 g | Salt: approx. 0.9 g

BUTTERNUT SQUASH AND LENTIL CURRY

A hearty and flavorful vegetarian curry made with tender butternut squash, protein-rich lentils, and a blend of aromatic spices. Perfect for a warming and satisfying meal.

Portions: 4 | **Difficulty Level:** Easy | **Preparation Time:** 15 minutes | **Cooking Time:** 30 minutes | **Total Time:** 45 minutes

INGREDIENTS:

- 1 medium butternut squash, peeled and diced
- 200 g red lentils, rinsed
- 1 can (400 ml) coconut milk
- 1 onion, finely chopped
- 3 cloves garlic, minced
- 1 tablespoon fresh ginger, grated
- 2 tablespoons curry powder
- 1 teaspoon ground cumin
- 1 teaspoon ground turmeric
- 1 tablespoon olive oil
- 600 ml vegetable broth
- 1 tablespoon fresh coriander, chopped (for garnish)
- Salt and freshly ground black pepper to taste
- Lemon wedges for serving

INSTRUCTIONS:

1. **Sauté the onion and spices:** In a large pot, heat the olive oil over medium heat. Add the chopped onion, garlic, and ginger, and sauté for 3-4 minutes until softened. Stir in the curry powder, cumin, and turmeric, and cook for 1 minute until fragrant.
2. **Add the butternut squash and lentils:** Add the diced butternut squash and red lentils to the pot, stirring to coat them in the spice mixture.
3. **Add the liquids:** Pour in the vegetable broth and coconut milk, stirring well. Bring the mixture to a boil, then reduce the heat to low and simmer for 25-30 minutes, or until the butternut squash is tender and the lentils are cooked through.
4. **Season and serve:** Taste and season the curry with salt and freshly ground black pepper. Serve the curry hot, garnished with fresh coriander and lemon wedges on the side. This curry pairs perfectly with rice, naan, or crusty bread.

ESTIMATED NUTRITIONAL INFORMATION PER SERVING:
Calories: approx. 350 kcal | Fat: approx. 15 g | Carbohydrates: approx. 40 g | Protein: approx. 12 g | Salt: approx. 1.0 g

CHAPTER 5: MAIN COURSES - SEAFOOD

Mediterranean seafood dishes using local UK fish and shellfish, focusing on light, fresh, and healthy options.

GRILLED SEA BASS WITH LEMON AND CAPERS

Fresh sea bass grilled to perfection and finished with a bright, tangy lemon and caper sauce.

Portions: 4 | **Difficulty Level:** Easy | **Preparation Time:** 10 minutes | **Cooking Time:** 15 minutes | **Total Time:** 25 minutes

INGREDIENTS:
- 4 sea bass fillets, skin on
- 2 tablespoons olive oil
- 2 tablespoons capers, rinsed
- 1 lemon, juice and zest
- 2 cloves garlic, minced
- Salt and freshly ground black pepper to taste
- Fresh parsley, chopped, for garnish

INSTRUCTIONS:
1. **Prepare the sea bass:** Rub the sea bass fillets with 1 tablespoon of olive oil and season both sides with salt and pepper. The skin should be lightly oiled to prevent sticking to the grill.
2. **Grill the sea bass:** Preheat a grill or grill pan over medium-high heat. Place the sea bass fillets skin-side down on the grill and cook for about 4-5 minutes, until the skin is crispy. Flip and cook for another 3-4 minutes, until the flesh is opaque and flakes easily with a fork. Be careful not to overcook the fish to retain its delicate texture.
3. **Make the lemon and caper sauce:** While the fish is grilling, heat the remaining olive oil in a small skillet over medium heat. Add the minced garlic and sauté for 1-2 minutes until fragrant. Stir in the capers, lemon juice, and lemon zest, cooking for another minute. Remove from heat.
4. **Serve:** Place the grilled sea bass fillets on a serving plate and spoon the lemon and caper sauce over the top. Garnish with fresh parsley and serve immediately. This dish pairs well with roasted vegetables or a light green salad.

ESTIMATED NUTRITIONAL INFORMATION PER SERVING:
Calories: approx. 250 kcal | Fat: approx. 15 g | Carbohydrates: approx. 2 g | Protein: approx. 28 g | Salt: approx. 0.8 g

SEAFOOD PAELLA WITH LOCAL MUSSELS AND PRAWNS

A classic Spanish dish packed with fresh mussels, prawns, and a saffron-infused rice base.

Portions: 4 | **Difficulty Level:** Medium | **Preparation Time:** 15 minutes | **Cooking Time:** 40 minutes | **Total Time:** 55 minutes

INGREDIENTS:

- 200 g prawns, peeled and deveined
- 200 g mussels, cleaned
- 300 g paella rice (such as Bomba or Calasparra)
- 1 large onion, finely chopped
- 2 cloves garlic, minced
- 1 red bell pepper, diced
- 2 ripe tomatoes, grated
- 1 teaspoon smoked paprika
- 1/4 teaspoon saffron threads, soaked in 2 tablespoons warm water
- 750 ml fish or vegetable broth, warmed
- 2 tablespoons olive oil
- Salt and freshly ground black pepper to taste
- Fresh parsley, chopped for garnish
- Lemon wedges for serving

INSTRUCTIONS:

1. **Sauté the vegetables:** Heat the olive oil in a large paella pan or wide, shallow pan over medium heat. Add the chopped onion, garlic, and diced red bell pepper, and sauté until softened, about 5-7 minutes. Stir in the grated tomatoes and cook for another 3 minutes.
2. **Add the spices and rice:** Stir in the smoked paprika and saffron (with its soaking liquid). Add the paella rice and stir to coat the grains in the flavorful oil and spices. Cook for 2-3 minutes, allowing the rice to absorb the flavours.
3. **Cook the paella:** Gradually add the warmed broth to the rice, stirring briefly to combine. Season with salt and pepper. Lower the heat to medium-low and simmer the paella uncovered, without stirring, for 15-20 minutes, or until the rice is almost fully cooked and the liquid has mostly absorbed. Resist the temptation to stir the rice—this helps develop the traditional crispy bottom known as "socarrat."
4. **Add the seafood:** Scatter the prawns and mussels over the top of the rice. Cover the pan with a lid or foil and cook for an additional 10 minutes, or until the prawns are pink and cooked through and the mussels have opened. Discard any mussels that remain closed.
5. **Serve:** Remove the pan from the heat and let the paella rest for 5 minutes. Garnish with fresh parsley and serve with lemon wedges. This dish is perfect for sharing and brings a taste of the Mediterranean to your table.

ESTIMATED NUTRITIONAL INFORMATION PER SERVING:
Calories: approx. 450 kcal | Fat: approx. 12 g | Carbohydrates: approx. 55 g | Protein: approx. 25 g | Salt: approx. 1.2 g

ROASTED COD WITH TOMATOES, GARLIC, AND OLIVES

Fresh cod fillets roasted with juicy tomatoes, garlic, and briny olives for a light and satisfying meal.

Portions: 4 | **Difficulty Level:** Easy | **Preparation Time:** 10 minutes | **Cooking Time:** 20 minutes | **Total Time:** 30 minutes

INGREDIENTS:

- 4 cod fillets (about 150-200 g each)
- 200 g cherry tomatoes, halved
- 2 cloves garlic, thinly sliced
- 100 g Kalamata olives, pitted and halved
- 2 tablespoons olive oil
- 1 lemon, zest and juice
- Salt and freshly ground black pepper to taste
- Fresh parsley, chopped for garnish

INSTRUCTIONS:

1. **Preheat the oven:** Preheat your oven to 200°C (400°F).
2. **Prepare the baking dish:** In a baking dish, scatter the cherry tomatoes, garlic slices, and olives. Drizzle with 1 tablespoon of olive oil, and season with salt and pepper. Toss gently to coat the vegetables in the oil and seasoning.
3. **Roast the tomatoes and olives:** Place the dish in the preheated oven and roast the tomatoes, garlic, and olives for about 10 minutes, or until the tomatoes begin to soften and release their juices.
4. **Add the cod fillets:** Remove the dish from the oven and place the cod fillets on top of the roasted vegetables. Drizzle the remaining olive oil and lemon juice over the fish, and season with a little more salt and pepper.
5. **Roast the cod:** Return the dish to the oven and roast for another 10-12 minutes, or until the cod is opaque and flakes easily with a fork. The cooking time may vary depending on the thickness of the fillets.
6. **Serve:** Garnish the roasted cod with freshly chopped parsley and lemon zest before serving. Serve the fish and vegetables with crusty bread or over a bed of rice or couscous. The bright flavours of the tomatoes and olives complement the tender cod beautifully.

ESTIMATED NUTRITIONAL INFORMATION PER SERVING:
Calories: approx. 300 kcal | Fat: approx. 14 g | Carbohydrates: approx. 6 g | Protein: approx. 35 g | Salt: approx. 1.0 g

SARDINES WITH A CITRUS AND HERB CRUST

Crispy sardines coated in a citrus and herb crust, baked until golden. Served with a fresh salad, they make for a quick and healthy seafood dish.

Portions: 4 | **Difficulty Level:** Easy | **Preparation Time:** 10 minutes | **Cooking Time:** 15 minutes | **Total Time:** 25 minutes

INGREDIENTS:
- 8 fresh sardines, cleaned and gutted
- 1 lemon, zest and juice
- 2 cloves garlic, minced
- 2 tablespoons fresh parsley, finely chopped
- 2 tablespoons fresh breadcrumbs
- 1 tablespoon olive oil
- Salt and freshly ground black pepper to taste
- Lemon wedges, for serving

INSTRUCTIONS:
1. **Preheat the oven:** Preheat your oven to 200°C (400°F) and line a baking tray with parchment paper.
2. **Prepare the crust:** In a small bowl, mix together the lemon zest, minced garlic, chopped parsley, breadcrumbs, olive oil, salt, and pepper until well combined.
3. **Season the sardines:** Lay the cleaned sardines on the prepared baking tray. Drizzle with lemon juice and season with a little salt and pepper.
4. **Top with the herb crust:** Spoon the citrus and herb mixture evenly over the top of each sardine, pressing lightly to adhere the crumbs to the fish.
5. **Bake the sardines:** Place the tray in the oven and bake for 12-15 minutes, or until the sardines are golden and crispy on the outside and cooked through. The sardines should be tender, and the crust should be crunchy and fragrant.
6. **Serve:** Serve the sardines immediately, with extra lemon wedges on the side for squeezing over. This dish pairs well with a fresh green salad or roasted vegetables for a light and healthy meal.

ESTIMATED NUTRITIONAL INFORMATION PER SERVING:
Calories: approx. 250 kcal | Fat: approx. 12 g | Carbohydrates: approx. 4 g | Protein: approx. 30 g | Salt: approx. 0.7 g

BAKED SALMON WITH DILL AND LEMON

A simple yet flavorful dish, with fresh salmon fillets baked in the oven and topped with a dill and lemon sauce, perfect for a light meal.

Portions: 4 | **Difficulty Level:** Easy | **Preparation Time:** 5 minutes | **Cooking Time:** 15 minutes | **Total Time:** 20 minutes

INGREDIENTS:
- 4 salmon fillets (about 150-200 g each)
- 1 lemon, thinly sliced
- 2 tablespoons fresh dill, chopped
- 2 tablespoons olive oil
- Salt and freshly ground black pepper to taste
- Lemon wedges for serving

INSTRUCTIONS:
1. **Preheat the oven:** Preheat your oven to 200°C (400°F). Line a baking tray with parchment paper.
2. **Prepare the salmon:** Place the salmon fillets on the prepared baking tray. Drizzle with olive oil and season with salt and pepper. Lay a few lemon slices over each fillet and sprinkle with chopped dill.
3. **Bake the salmon:** Bake the salmon in the preheated oven for 12-15 minutes, or until the salmon is opaque and flakes easily with a fork. Cooking time may vary depending on the thickness of the fillets.
4. **Serve:** Serve the baked salmon with extra lemon wedges on the side for squeezing over. This light and flavorful dish pairs beautifully with steamed vegetables or a fresh green salad.

ESTIMATED NUTRITIONAL INFORMATION PER SERVING:
Calories: approx. 300 kcal | Fat: approx. 18 g | Carbohydrates: approx. 2 g | Protein: approx. 30 g | Salt: approx. 0.5 g

PRAWNS WITH GARLIC, CHILI, AND LEMON

Succulent prawns sautéed with garlic, fresh chilli, and a splash of lemon, delivering a burst of flavours in every bite.

Portions: 4 | **Difficulty Level:** Easy | **Preparation Time:** 10 minutes | **Cooking Time:** 5 minutes | **Total Time:** 15 minutes

INGREDIENTS:

- 400 g prawns, peeled and deveined
- 3 cloves garlic, minced
- 1 red chilli, finely chopped (adjust to taste)
- 1 lemon, zest and juice
- 3 tablespoons olive oil
- Salt and freshly ground black pepper to taste
- Fresh parsley, chopped for garnish

INSTRUCTIONS:

1. **Heat the oil:** In a large skillet, heat the olive oil over medium heat. Add the minced garlic and chopped chilli, cooking for 1-2 minutes until fragrant but not browned.
2. **Cook the prawns:** Add the prawns to the skillet, cooking for 2-3 minutes on each side, or until they turn pink and opaque. Be careful not to overcook the prawns, as they can become tough.
3. **Add lemon:** Remove the skillet from the heat and stir in the lemon zest and juice. Season with salt and freshly ground black pepper to taste.
4. **Serve:** Transfer the prawns to a serving plate and garnish with freshly chopped parsley. Serve with crusty bread or over a bed of rice to soak up the flavorful sauce. This dish is perfect for a quick and tasty appetiser or light meal.

ESTIMATED NUTRITIONAL INFORMATION PER SERVING:
Calories: approx. 200 kcal | Fat: approx. 12 g | Carbohydrates: approx. 2 g | Protein: approx. 22 g | Salt: approx. 0.8 g

OCTOPUS SALAD WITH POTATOES AND CAPERS

Tender octopus combined with boiled potatoes, capers, and fresh herbs, tossed in olive oil for a Mediterranean-inspired seafood salad.

Portions: 4 | **Difficulty Level:** Medium | **Preparation Time:** 15 minutes | **Cooking Time:** 1 hour (for the octopus) | **Total Time:** 1 hour 15 minutes

INGREDIENTS:

- 500 g octopus, cleaned
- 500 g potatoes, peeled and cut into chunks
- 2 tablespoons capers, rinsed
- 1 small red onion, thinly sliced
- 2 tablespoons fresh parsley, chopped
- 3 tablespoons extra virgin olive oil
- Juice of 1 lemon
- Salt and freshly ground black pepper to taste

INSTRUCTIONS:

1. **Cook the octopus:** Bring a large pot of salted water to a boil. Add the cleaned octopus, reduce the heat, and simmer for 45 minutes to 1 hour, or until the octopus is tender. Remove from the water and let cool. Once cooled, chop the octopus into bite-sized pieces.
2. **Cook the potatoes:** While the octopus is cooking, boil the potatoes in salted water for about 15 minutes, or until tender. Drain and let them cool slightly.
3. **Assemble the salad:** In a large mixing bowl, combine the chopped octopus, boiled potatoes, capers, and thinly sliced red onion.
4. **Dress the salad:** In a small bowl, whisk together the olive oil and lemon juice. Pour the dressing over the salad, and toss gently to combine. Season with salt and freshly ground black pepper to taste.
5. **Serve:** Garnish the salad with freshly chopped parsley and serve at room temperature or slightly chilled. This Mediterranean-inspired salad pairs well with a crisp white wine and is perfect as a light main course or appetiser.

ESTIMATED NUTRITIONAL INFORMATION PER SERVING:
Calories: approx. 300 kcal | Fat: approx. 15 g | Carbohydrates: approx. 30 g | Protein: approx. 15 g | Salt: approx. 1.0 g

TUNA STEAKS WITH A SUN-DRIED TOMATO AND OLIVE TAPENADE

Seared tuna steaks topped with a flavorful tapenade of sun-dried tomatoes, olives, and capers, making for an elegant seafood dinner.

Portions: 4 | **Difficulty Level:** Medium | **Preparation Time:** 10 minutes | **Cooking Time:** 8 minutes | **Total Time:** 18 minutes

INGREDIENTS:
- 4 tuna steaks (about 150-200 g each)
- 100 g sun-dried tomatoes, finely chopped
- 50 g Kalamata olives, pitted and chopped
- 1 tablespoon capers, rinsed
- 1 tablespoon fresh parsley, chopped
- 2 cloves garlic, minced
- 2 tablespoons olive oil
- Juice of 1 lemon
- Salt and freshly ground black pepper to taste

INSTRUCTIONS:
1. **Prepare the tapenade:** In a small bowl, combine the chopped sun-dried tomatoes, Kalamata olives, capers, parsley, and minced garlic. Stir in 1 tablespoon of olive oil and lemon juice. Mix well and set aside.
2. **Season the tuna steaks:** Rub the tuna steaks with the remaining 1 tablespoon of olive oil and season both sides with salt and freshly ground black pepper.
3. **Sear the tuna steaks:** Heat a large skillet or grill pan over medium-high heat. Sear the tuna steaks for about 2-3 minutes on each side, depending on thickness, for medium-rare. If you prefer the tuna well-done, cook for an additional minute on each side, but be careful not to overcook, as tuna can become dry.
4. **Serve:** Place the seared tuna steaks on a serving plate and top with the sun-dried tomato and olive tapenade. Serve immediately with a side of roasted vegetables or a green salad. This dish pairs wonderfully with a glass of crisp white wine or a light Mediterranean side dish.

ESTIMATED NUTRITIONAL INFORMATION PER SERVING:
Calories: approx. 350 kcal | Fat: approx. 18 g | Carbohydrates: approx. 4 g | Protein: approx. 40 g | Salt: approx. 1.2 g

SWORDFISH SKEWERS WITH PEPPERS AND ONIONS

Grilled swordfish skewers, paired with sweet peppers and onions, marinated in olive oil and fresh herbs for a light and satisfying dish.

Portions: 4 | **Difficulty Level:** Medium | **Preparation Time:** 15 minutes | **Cooking Time:** 10 minutes | **Total Time:** 25 minutes

INGREDIENTS:

- 500 g swordfish steaks, cut into 1-inch cubes
- 1 red bell pepper, cut into chunks
- 1 yellow bell pepper, cut into chunks
- 1 red onion, cut into chunks
- 2 tablespoons olive oil
- 2 tablespoons lemon juice
- 1 tablespoon fresh oregano, chopped
- Salt and freshly ground black pepper to taste
- Lemon wedges for serving

INSTRUCTIONS:

1. **Prepare the marinade:** In a small bowl, whisk together the olive oil, lemon juice, fresh oregano, salt, and pepper.
2. **Marinate the swordfish:** Place the swordfish cubes in a shallow dish and pour the marinade over them. Toss to coat and let sit for about 10-15 minutes while you prepare the vegetables.
3. **Assemble the skewers:** Thread the marinated swordfish cubes onto skewers, alternating with chunks of red and yellow bell pepper and onion.
4. **Grill the skewers:** Preheat a grill or grill pan over medium-high heat. Cook the skewers for 8-10 minutes, turning occasionally, until the swordfish is cooked through and the vegetables are slightly charred. Be careful not to overcook the swordfish, as it can become tough.
5. **Serve:** Transfer the skewers to a serving plate and garnish with lemon wedges for squeezing over the top. These swordfish skewers are perfectly served with a side of couscous or a fresh salad for a light and flavorful meal.

ESTIMATED NUTRITIONAL INFORMATION PER SERVING:
Calories: approx. 280 kcal | Fat: approx. 12 g | Carbohydrates: approx. 6 g | Protein: approx. 35 g | Salt: approx. 0.8 g

CLAMS IN A WHITE WINE AND GARLIC BROTH

Fresh clams cooked in a fragrant white wine and garlic broth, served with crusty bread to soak up the delicious juices.

Portions: 4 | **Difficulty Level:** Easy | **Preparation Time:** 10 minutes | **Cooking Time:** 10 minutes | **Total Time:** 20 minutes

INGREDIENTS:

- 1 kg fresh clams, scrubbed and cleaned
- 3 cloves garlic, minced
- 1 small shallot, finely chopped
- 200 ml dry white wine
- 2 tablespoons olive oil
- 1 tablespoon butter
- Fresh parsley, chopped, for garnish
- Lemon wedges for serving
- Salt and freshly ground black pepper to taste
- Crusty bread for serving

INSTRUCTIONS:

1. **Sauté the garlic and shallot:** In a large, deep skillet or pot, heat the olive oil and butter over medium heat. Add the minced garlic and chopped shallot, sautéing for 2-3 minutes until softened and fragrant.
2. **Add the white wine:** Pour in the white wine and bring to a simmer. Allow the wine to cook for about 2-3 minutes, reducing slightly.
3. **Cook the clams:** Add the cleaned clams to the pot, cover with a lid, and cook for 5-7 minutes, or until the clams have opened. Discard any clams that do not open after cooking.
4. **Season and garnish:** Remove the pot from the heat and season with salt and freshly ground black pepper to taste. Stir in the chopped parsley.
5. **Serve:** Serve the clams in the white wine and garlic broth with crusty bread on the side for dipping. Garnish with lemon wedges for an extra burst of freshness. This dish makes a delicious appetiser or light meal, perfect for soaking up the flavorful broth.

ESTIMATED NUTRITIONAL INFORMATION PER SERVING:
Calories: approx. 250 kcal | Fat: approx. 12 g | Carbohydrates: approx. 10 g | Protein: approx. 20 g | Salt: approx. 1.2 g

EXCLUSIVE BONUS

40 Weight Loss Recipes

&

14 Days Meal Plan

Scan the QR-Code and receive the FREE download:

CHAPTER 6: MAIN COURSES - MEAT

Traditional Mediterranean meat dishes, showcasing lamb, chicken, and other proteins, combined with fresh herbs and spices.

LAMB KOFTA WITH MINT YOGURT AND CUCUMBER SALAD

Tender and flavorful lamb kofta, grilled to perfection and served with a cooling mint yoghourt sauce and fresh cucumber salad.

Portions: 4 | **Difficulty Level:** Medium | **Preparation Time:** 20 minutes | **Cooking Time:** 10 minutes | **Total Time:** 30 minutes

INGREDIENTS:

For the Lamb Kofta:
- 500 g ground lamb
- 1 small onion, finely chopped
- 2 cloves garlic, minced
- 1 teaspoon ground cumin
- 1 teaspoon ground coriander
- 1/2 teaspoon ground cinnamon
- 1/2 teaspoon paprika
- Salt and freshly ground black pepper to taste
- 2 tablespoons fresh parsley, chopped
- Olive oil for grilling

For the Mint Yogurt:
- 200 g Greek yoghourt
- 1 tablespoon fresh mint, chopped
- 1 tablespoon lemon juice
- Salt and freshly ground black pepper to taste

For the Cucumber Salad:
- 1 large cucumber, sliced
- 1 tablespoon olive oil
- 1 tablespoon lemon juice
- Fresh mint leaves for garnish
- Salt and freshly ground black pepper to taste

INSTRUCTIONS:

1. **Prepare the lamb kofta:** In a large bowl, combine the ground lamb, chopped onion, minced garlic, cumin, coriander, cinnamon, paprika, salt, pepper, and parsley. Mix well until the ingredients are fully incorporated. Form the mixture into small, oval-shaped kofta patties or shape them onto skewers.
2. **Cook the kofta:** Heat a grill or grill pan over medium-high heat. Brush the kofta with a little olive oil and grill for about 4-5 minutes on each side, or until cooked through and nicely browned. The kofta should have a slightly charred exterior and be juicy on the inside.
3. **Make the mint yoghourt:** In a small bowl, mix together the Greek yoghourt, chopped mint, lemon juice, salt, and pepper. Stir well and adjust seasoning to taste. Set aside.
4. **Prepare the cucumber salad:** In a separate bowl, toss the cucumber slices with olive oil, lemon juice, salt, and pepper. Garnish with fresh mint leaves.
5. **Serve:** Serve the grilled lamb kofta with a generous dollop of mint yoghourt and the cucumber salad on the side. This dish pairs perfectly with warm flatbread or a side of couscous.

ESTIMATED NUTRITIONAL INFORMATION PER SERVING:
Calories: approx. 450 kcal | Fat: approx. 30 g | Carbohydrates: approx. 8 g | Protein: approx. 35 g | Salt: approx. 0.8 g

GRILLED CHICKEN WITH LEMON AND THYME MARINADE

Juicy grilled chicken marinated in fresh lemon juice and thyme, giving it a burst of flavour with every bite. Serve with roasted vegetables for a complete meal.

Portions: 4 | **Difficulty Level:** Easy | **Preparation Time:** 10 minutes (plus marinating time) | **Cooking Time:** 15 minutes | **Total Time:** 25 minutes (plus marinating)

INGREDIENTS:
- 4 boneless, skinless chicken breasts
- 3 tablespoons olive oil
- Juice and zest of 1 lemon
- 2 cloves garlic, minced
- 2 tablespoons fresh thyme leaves, chopped
- Salt and freshly ground black pepper to taste
- Lemon wedges, for serving

INSTRUCTIONS:
1. **Prepare the marinade:** In a small bowl, whisk together the olive oil, lemon juice, lemon zest, minced garlic, chopped thyme, salt, and pepper.
2. **Marinate the chicken:** Place the chicken breasts in a shallow dish or resealable plastic bag. Pour the marinade over the chicken, ensuring each piece is well-coated. Let the chicken marinate in the refrigerator for at least 30 minutes, or up to 2 hours for more flavour. Marinating allows the lemon and thyme to infuse the chicken with a fresh, aromatic flavour.
3. **Grill the chicken:** Preheat a grill or grill pan over medium-high heat. Remove the chicken from the marinade and grill for about 6-7 minutes on each side, or until the chicken is cooked through and has nice grill marks. The internal temperature should reach 75°C (165°F) when fully cooked.
4. **Serve:** Serve the grilled chicken with lemon wedges for squeezing over the top. This dish pairs perfectly with roasted vegetables, rice, or a light salad.

ESTIMATED NUTRITIONAL INFORMATION PER SERVING:
Calories: approx. 280 kcal | Fat: approx. 12 g | Carbohydrates: approx. 3 g | Protein: approx. 40 g | Salt: approx. 0.6 g

SLOW-COOKED LAMB TAGINE WITH APRICOTS AND ALMONDS

This traditional Moroccan dish features tender lamb cooked slowly with apricots, almonds, and warm spices, resulting in a fragrant, sweet, and savoury stew.

Portions: 4 | **Difficulty Level:** Medium | **Preparation Time:** 20 minutes | **Cooking Time:** 2 hours | **Total Time:** 2 hours 20 minutes

INGREDIENTS:

- 800 g lamb shoulder, cut into large chunks
- 1 onion, finely chopped
- 2 cloves garlic, minced
- 200 g dried apricots, halved
- 50 g almonds, toasted
- 1 teaspoon ground cumin
- 1 teaspoon ground cinnamon
- 1 teaspoon ground ginger
- 1 teaspoon ground coriander
- 1/2 teaspoon turmeric
- 1/4 teaspoon cayenne pepper (optional)
- 400 ml beef or lamb broth
- 2 tablespoons olive oil
- Fresh cilantro, chopped for garnish
- Salt and freshly ground black pepper to taste

INSTRUCTIONS:

1. **Brown the lamb:** In a large, heavy-bottomed pot or tagine, heat the olive oil over medium-high heat. Season the lamb with salt and pepper, and brown the lamb chunks on all sides, about 5-7 minutes. Remove the lamb and set aside.
2. **Cook the onions and garlic:** In the same pot, add the chopped onions and cook for 3-4 minutes until softened. Add the minced garlic and cook for another minute.
3. **Add the spices:** Stir in the cumin, cinnamon, ginger, coriander, turmeric, and cayenne pepper (if using). Cook the spices for 1-2 minutes to release their aroma.
4. **Simmer the tagine:** Return the browned lamb to the pot. Add the dried apricots and broth. Bring the mixture to a simmer, cover the pot, and lower the heat. Cook for 1.5 to 2 hours, or until the lamb is tender and the flavours are well-developed.
5. **Finish and serve:** Once the lamb is tender, stir in the toasted almonds. Adjust seasoning with salt and pepper, if needed. Garnish with freshly chopped cilantro and serve with couscous or flatbread.

ESTIMATED NUTRITIONAL INFORMATION PER SERVING:
Calories: approx. 500 kcal | Fat: approx. 25 g | Carbohydrates: approx. 40 g | Protein: approx. 30 g | Salt: approx. 1.0 g

SPICED MEATBALLS IN A RICH TOMATO SAUCE

Juicy meatballs made with a blend of Mediterranean spices, simmered in a rich tomato sauce. Perfect for serving over pasta or with fresh bread for dipping.

Portions: 4 | **Difficulty Level:** Medium | **Preparation Time:** 15 minutes | **Cooking Time:** 30 minutes | **Total Time:** 45 minutes

INGREDIENTS:

For the Meatballs:
- 500 g ground beef or lamb
- 1 small onion, finely chopped
- 2 cloves garlic, minced
- 1 teaspoon ground cumin
- 1 teaspoon ground coriander
- 1/2 teaspoon smoked paprika
- 1/4 teaspoon ground cinnamon
- Salt and freshly ground black pepper to taste
- 2 tablespoons fresh parsley, chopped
- 1 egg, lightly beaten
- 2 tablespoons breadcrumbs

For the Tomato Sauce:
- 1 can (400 g) chopped tomatoes
- 1 tablespoon tomato paste
- 1 onion, finely chopped
- 2 cloves garlic, minced
- 1 teaspoon sugar
- 1 teaspoon dried oregano
- 2 tablespoons olive oil
- Salt and freshly ground black pepper to taste
- Fresh basil leaves for garnish (optional)

INSTRUCTIONS:

1. **Prepare the meatballs:** In a large bowl, mix together the ground beef or lamb, chopped onion, minced garlic, cumin, coriander, smoked paprika, cinnamon, salt, pepper, parsley, egg, and breadcrumbs. Combine well and form the mixture into small meatballs, about the size of a walnut.
2. **Brown the meatballs:** In a large skillet, heat 1 tablespoon of olive oil over medium-high heat. Add the meatballs and cook for 4-5 minutes, turning occasionally until browned on all sides. Remove from the skillet and set aside.
3. **Make the tomato sauce:** In the same skillet, heat the remaining tablespoon of olive oil over medium heat. Add the chopped onion and garlic and sauté for 3-4 minutes until softened. Stir in the chopped tomatoes, tomato paste, sugar, oregano, salt, and pepper. Bring the sauce to a simmer and cook for 10 minutes, allowing the flavours to develop.
4. **Simmer the meatballs:** Return the browned meatballs to the skillet with the tomato sauce. Cover and simmer for 15-20 minutes, or until the meatballs are cooked through and the sauce has thickened.
5. **Serve:** Garnish the dish with fresh basil leaves if desired. Serve the meatballs and sauce over pasta, with crusty bread, or on their own as a hearty main course.

ESTIMATED NUTRITIONAL INFORMATION PER SERVING:
Calories: approx. 450 kcal | Fat: approx. 25 g | Carbohydrates: approx. 20 g | Protein: approx. 35 g | Salt: approx. 1.2 g

GRILLED LAMB CHOPS WITH ROSEMARY AND GARLIC

Juicy lamb chops grilled to perfection, marinated with rosemary, garlic, and a touch of lemon for an extra burst of flavour.

Portions: 4 | **Difficulty Level:** Easy | **Preparation Time:** 10 minutes (plus marinating time) | **Cooking Time:** 10 minutes | **Total Time:** 20 minutes (plus marinating)

INGREDIENTS:
- 8 lamb chops
- 3 cloves garlic, minced
- 2 tablespoons fresh rosemary, chopped
- Juice and zest of 1 lemon
- 3 tablespoons olive oil
- Salt and freshly ground black pepper to taste
- Lemon wedges for serving

INSTRUCTIONS:
1. **Prepare the marinade:** In a small bowl, mix together the minced garlic, chopped rosemary, lemon juice, lemon zest, olive oil, salt, and pepper.
2. **Marinate the lamb chops:** Place the lamb chops in a shallow dish or resealable plastic bag. Pour the marinade over the lamb chops, ensuring each chop is coated. Marinate in the refrigerator for at least 30 minutes, or up to 2 hours for more flavour.
3. **Grill the lamb chops:** Preheat a grill or grill pan over medium-high heat. Remove the lamb chops from the marinade and grill for about 4-5 minutes on each side, or until they reach your desired level of doneness. For medium-rare, the internal temperature should be around 60°C (140°F).
4. **Serve:** Transfer the lamb chops to a serving plate and let them rest for a few minutes. Serve with lemon wedges for squeezing over the top. These lamb chops pair beautifully with roasted vegetables, potatoes, or a light salad.

ESTIMATED NUTRITIONAL INFORMATION PER SERVING:
Calories: approx. 400 kcal | Fat: approx. 30 g | Carbohydrates: approx. 3 g | Protein: approx. 25 g | Salt: approx. 0.7 g

CHICKEN SHAWARMA WITH A SPICED YOGURT MARINADE

Thinly sliced marinated chicken, packed with Mediterranean spices and grilled until tender. Served with warm flatbread and a side of fresh vegetables.

Portions: 4 | **Difficulty Level:** Medium | **Preparation Time:** 15 minutes (plus marinating time) | **Cooking Time:** 20 minutes | **Total Time:** 35 minutes (plus marinating)

INGREDIENTS:

- 4 boneless, skinless chicken thighs
- 200 g Greek yoghourt
- 2 cloves garlic, minced
- 2 tablespoons lemon juice
- 1 teaspoon ground cumin
- 1 teaspoon ground coriander
- 1/2 teaspoon ground paprika
- 1/2 teaspoon ground turmeric
- 1/4 teaspoon ground cinnamon
- 1/4 teaspoon cayenne pepper (optional)
- Salt and freshly ground black pepper to taste
- 2 tablespoons olive oil
- Fresh parsley, chopped for garnish
- Warm flatbread for serving

INSTRUCTIONS:

1. **Prepare the marinade:** In a bowl, whisk together the Greek yoghourt, minced garlic, lemon juice, cumin, coriander, paprika, turmeric, cinnamon, cayenne pepper (if using), salt, and pepper.
2. **Marinate the chicken:** Place the chicken thighs in a shallow dish or resealable plastic bag. Pour the yoghourt marinade over the chicken, making sure each piece is well-coated. Marinate in the refrigerator for at least 1 hour, or up to 4 hours for the best flavour.
3. **Cook the chicken:** Heat the olive oil in a large skillet over medium-high heat. Remove the chicken from the marinade and cook for 6-8 minutes on each side, or until the chicken is golden brown and cooked through. The internal temperature should reach 75°C (165°F).
4. **Serve:** Slice the cooked chicken into strips and serve in warm flatbread with fresh parsley and any additional toppings of your choice, such as cucumber, tomato, or pickled vegetables. This dish pairs well with a side of hummus, baba ganoush, or a cucumber salad.

ESTIMATED NUTRITIONAL INFORMATION PER SERVING:
Calories: approx. 350 kcal | Fat: approx. 20 g | Carbohydrates: approx. 8 g | Protein: approx. 30 g | Salt: approx. 1.0 g

BEEF SOUVLAKI SKEWERS WITH TZATZIKI

Tender chunks of beef, marinated in olive oil and herbs, grilled on skewers and served with a refreshing tzatziki sauce.

Portions: 4 | **Difficulty Level:** Medium | **Preparation Time:** 15 minutes (plus marinating time) | **Cooking Time:** 10 minutes | **Total Time:** 25 minutes (plus marinating)

INGREDIENTS:

For the Beef Souvlaki:
- 500 g beef sirloin, cut into 1-inch cubes
- 2 tablespoons olive oil
- Juice of 1 lemon
- 2 cloves garlic, minced
- 1 tablespoon dried oregano
- Salt and freshly ground black pepper to taste
- Wooden skewers, soaked in water for 30 minutes

For the Tzatziki:
- 200 g Greek yoghourt
- 1/2 cucumber, grated and squeezed to remove excess water
- 1 clove garlic, minced
- 1 tablespoon olive oil
- 1 tablespoon fresh dill, chopped
- Juice of 1/2 lemon
- Salt and freshly ground black pepper to taste

INSTRUCTIONS:

1. **Marinate the beef:** In a large bowl, combine the olive oil, lemon juice, minced garlic, oregano, salt, and pepper. Add the beef cubes and toss to coat. Marinate in the refrigerator for at least 1 hour, or up to 4 hours for the best flavour.
2. **Prepare the tzatziki:** While the beef marinades, make the tzatziki by combining the Greek yoghourt, grated cucumber, minced garlic, olive oil, fresh dill, lemon juice, salt, and pepper in a small bowl. Stir well and refrigerate until ready to serve.
3. **Assemble the skewers:** Thread the marinated beef cubes onto the soaked wooden skewers.
4. **Grill the beef:** Preheat a grill or grill pan over medium-high heat. Grill the beef skewers for 8-10 minutes, turning occasionally, until the beef is cooked to your desired level of doneness. For medium-rare, the internal temperature should be about 60°C (140°F).
5. **Serve:** Serve the beef souvlaki skewers with a side of tzatziki and warm pita bread. This dish pairs beautifully with a Greek salad or roasted vegetables.

ESTIMATED NUTRITIONAL INFORMATION PER SERVING:
Calories: approx. 400 kcal | Fat: approx. 22 g | Carbohydrates: approx. 8 g | Protein: approx. 40 g | Salt: approx. 0.9 g

MOROCCAN CHICKEN WITH PRESERVED LEMONS AND OLIVES

A rich and flavorful chicken dish, slow-cooked with preserved lemons, olives, and a blend of Moroccan spices for a fragrant and hearty meal.

Portions: 4 | **Difficulty Level:** Medium | **Preparation Time:** 15 minutes | **Cooking Time:** 1 hour | **Total Time:** 1 hour 15 minutes

INGREDIENTS:

- 4 bone-in, skin-on chicken thighs
- 2 preserved lemons, rinsed and quartered
- 100 g green olives, pitted
- 1 onion, finely chopped
- 3 cloves garlic, minced
- 1 teaspoon ground cumin
- 1 teaspoon ground coriander
- 1/2 teaspoon ground turmeric
- 1/4 teaspoon ground cinnamon
- 1/4 teaspoon saffron threads (optional)
- 400 ml chicken broth
- 2 tablespoons olive oil
- Fresh cilantro, chopped for garnish
- Salt and freshly ground black pepper to taste

INSTRUCTIONS:

1. **Brown the chicken:** In a large, heavy-bottomed pot or tagine, heat the olive oil over medium-high heat. Season the chicken thighs with salt and pepper. Brown the chicken on both sides, about 4-5 minutes per side, until golden. Remove and set aside.
2. **Cook the onions and garlic:** In the same pot, add the chopped onion and cook for 3-4 minutes until softened. Add the minced garlic and cook for another minute, stirring frequently.
3. **Add the spices:** Stir in the cumin, coriander, turmeric, cinnamon, and saffron (if using). Cook the spices for 1-2 minutes to release their aroma.
4. **Simmer the chicken:** Return the browned chicken thighs to the pot. Add the preserved lemons, green olives, and chicken broth. Bring the mixture to a simmer, then cover and reduce the heat to low. Simmer gently for 45-50 minutes, or until the chicken is tender and cooked through.
5. **Finish and serve:** Adjust seasoning with salt and pepper if needed. Garnish with freshly chopped cilantro before serving. This fragrant dish pairs perfectly with couscous or rice to soak up the flavorful sauce.

ESTIMATED NUTRITIONAL INFORMATION PER SERVING:
Calories: approx. 450 kcal | Fat: approx. 28 g | Carbohydrates: approx. 8 g | Protein: approx. 35 g | Salt: approx. 1.2 g

ROAST PORK WITH GARLIC, ROSEMARY, AND LEMON

A succulent pork roast seasoned with garlic, fresh rosemary, and lemon, roasted until golden and tender.

Portions: 4 | **Difficulty Level:** Medium | **Preparation Time:** 10 minutes | **Cooking Time:** 1 hour 30 minutes | **Total Time:** 1 hour 40 minutes

INGREDIENTS:

- 1 kg boneless pork loin
- 4 cloves garlic, minced
- 2 tablespoons fresh rosemary, chopped
- Juice and zest of 1 lemon
- 3 tablespoons olive oil
- Salt and freshly ground black pepper to taste
- 1 cup chicken broth (optional)

INSTRUCTIONS:

1. **Preheat the oven:** Preheat your oven to 180°C (350°F).
2. **Prepare the marinade:** In a small bowl, mix together the minced garlic, chopped rosemary, lemon juice, lemon zest, olive oil, salt, and pepper to form a marinade.
3. **Marinate the pork:** Rub the pork loin all over with the garlic and rosemary marinade, ensuring it's well coated. Place the pork in a roasting pan, fat side up.
4. **Roast the pork:** Roast the pork in the preheated oven for 1 hour 30 minutes, or until the internal temperature reaches 70°C (160°F). Halfway through cooking, baste the pork with the juices from the pan. If the pan becomes too dry, you can add chicken broth to the pan for extra moisture.
5. **Rest and serve:** Once the pork is cooked, remove it from the oven and let it rest for 10 minutes before slicing. Serve with roasted vegetables or potatoes for a complete meal.

ESTIMATED NUTRITIONAL INFORMATION PER SERVING:
Calories: approx. 450 kcal | Fat: approx. 30 g | Carbohydrates: approx. 2 g | Protein: approx. 38 g | Salt: approx. 0.9 g

BRAISED BEEF WITH RED WINE AND THYME

Tender beef slow-cooked with red wine, garlic, and thyme, creating a rich and comforting dish perfect for cooler months.

Portions: 4 | **Difficulty Level:** Medium | **Preparation Time:** 15 minutes | **Cooking Time:** 2 hours 30 minutes | **Total Time:** 2 hours 45 minutes

INGREDIENTS:

- 800 g beef chuck, cut into large chunks
- 1 onion, finely chopped
- 3 cloves garlic, minced
- 2 carrots, sliced
- 2 celery stalks, chopped
- 500 ml red wine
- 300 ml beef broth
- 2 tablespoons tomato paste
- 2 sprigs fresh thyme
- 2 bay leaves
- 2 tablespoons olive oil
- Salt and freshly ground black pepper to taste

INSTRUCTIONS:

1. **Brown the beef:** In a large, heavy-bottomed pot, heat the olive oil over medium-high heat. Season the beef with salt and pepper, and brown the chunks on all sides, about 5-7 minutes. Remove the beef and set aside.
2. **Cook the vegetables:** In the same pot, add the chopped onion, garlic, carrots, and celery. Cook for 5-6 minutes until softened, stirring occasionally.
3. **Add the wine and broth:** Stir in the tomato paste and cook for 1 minute. Pour in the red wine, using a wooden spoon to scrape up any browned bits from the bottom of the pot. Bring to a simmer and let the wine reduce for 5 minutes.
4. **Simmer the beef:** Return the browned beef to the pot. Add the beef broth, thyme sprigs, and bay leaves. Bring the mixture to a simmer, cover the pot, and reduce the heat to low. Simmer gently for 2 to 2.5 hours, or until the beef is tender and the sauce has thickened.
5. **Serve:** Remove the thyme sprigs and bay leaves before serving. This rich and hearty braised beef is perfect served with mashed potatoes or crusty bread to soak up the flavorful sauce.

ESTIMATED NUTRITIONAL INFORMATION PER SERVING:

Calories: approx. 500 kcal | Fat: approx. 22 g | Carbohydrates: approx. 12 g | Protein: approx. 45 g | Salt: approx. 1.0 g

MOROCCAN-SPICED LAMB CHOPS WITH COUSCOUS

Tender lamb chops marinated in a fragrant blend of Moroccan spices, served with fluffy couscous and a drizzle of yogurt sauce. A hearty and flavorful main course that brings the taste of the Mediterranean to your table.

Portions: 4 | **Difficulty Level:** Medium | **Preparation Time:** 15 minutes (plus 30 minutes marinating time) | **Cooking Time:** 15 minutes | **Total Time:** 1 hour

INGREDIENTS:

For the Lamb Chops:
- 8 lamb chops
- 2 tablespoons olive oil
- 2 cloves garlic, minced
- 1 tablespoon ground cumin
- 1 teaspoon ground coriander
- 1 teaspoon paprika
- 1/2 teaspoon ground cinnamon
- 1/2 teaspoon cayenne pepper (optional)
- Salt and freshly ground black pepper to taste

For the Couscous:
- 200 g couscous
- 300 ml vegetable broth
- 1 tablespoon olive oil
- 1 tablespoon fresh mint, chopped
- 1 tablespoon fresh parsley, chopped
- Zest of 1 lemon

For the Yogurt Sauce:
- 150 g Greek yogurt
- 1 tablespoon fresh lemon juice
- 1 tablespoon fresh mint, chopped
- Salt and freshly ground black pepper to taste

INSTRUCTIONS:

1. **Marinate the lamb chops:** In a bowl, mix together the olive oil, minced garlic, cumin, coriander, paprika, cinnamon, cayenne pepper (if using), salt, and black pepper. Rub the lamb chops with the spice mixture and let them marinate for at least 30 minutes.
2. **Cook the couscous:** In a saucepan, bring the vegetable broth to a boil. Remove from heat, stir in the couscous, cover, and let it sit for 5 minutes. Fluff the couscous with a fork and stir in the olive oil, mint, parsley, and lemon zest. Set aside.
3. **Grill the lamb chops:** Heat a grill pan or skillet over medium-high heat. Cook the lamb chops for 3-4 minutes on each side, or until they reach your desired level of doneness. Let the lamb rest for a few minutes before serving.
4. **Prepare the yogurt sauce:** In a small bowl, whisk together the Greek yogurt, lemon juice, mint, salt, and black pepper.
5. **Serve:** Serve the grilled lamb chops over the couscous, with a drizzle of the yogurt sauce on top. Garnish with extra fresh herbs for a burst of color and flavor.

ESTIMATED NUTRITIONAL INFORMATION PER SERVING:
Calories: approx. 450 kcal | Fat: approx. 25 g | Carbohydrates: approx. 35 g | Protein: approx. 25 g | Salt: approx. 0.9 g

STUFFED CHICKEN BREASTS WITH SPINACH AND FETA

Juicy chicken breasts stuffed with a flavourful mixture of sautéed spinach, feta cheese, and fresh herbs. This Mediterranean-inspired dish is perfect for a hearty yet elegant main course.

Portions: 4 | **Difficulty Level:** Medium | **Preparation Time:** 20 minutes | **Cooking Time:** 25 minutes | **Total Time:** 45 minutes

INGREDIENTS:

- 4 boneless, skinless chicken breasts
- 150 g fresh spinach, sautéed and drained
- 100 g feta cheese, crumbled
- 2 cloves garlic, minced
- 1 tablespoon olive oil
- 1 tablespoon fresh parsley, chopped
- 1 teaspoon dried oregano
- Salt and freshly ground black pepper to taste
- Toothpicks (for sealing)

INSTRUCTIONS:

1. **Prepare the filling:** In a small bowl, combine the sautéed spinach, crumbled feta, minced garlic, parsley, oregano, and a pinch of salt and black pepper. Mix well.
2. **Butterfly the chicken breasts:** Using a sharp knife, carefully slice each chicken breast horizontally to create a pocket, being careful not to cut all the way through.
3. **Stuff the chicken breasts:** Spoon the spinach and feta mixture into the pocket of each chicken breast. Use toothpicks to secure the edges and keep the filling in place.
4. **Season the chicken:** Rub the outside of the stuffed chicken breasts with olive oil and season with salt and black pepper.
5. **Cook the chicken:** Heat a large oven-safe skillet over medium heat and sear the stuffed chicken breasts for 3-4 minutes on each side until golden. Transfer the skillet to a preheated oven at 180°C (350°F) and bake for 15-20 minutes, or until the chicken is cooked through and the filling is hot and bubbly.
6. **Serve:** Remove the toothpicks and serve the stuffed chicken breasts with a side of rice, couscous, or a fresh salad. This dish pairs beautifully with a drizzle of olive oil or a squeeze of fresh lemon.

ESTIMATED NUTRITIONAL INFORMATION PER SERVING:
Calories: approx. 350 kcal | Fat: approx. 18 g | Carbohydrates: approx. 3 g | Protein: approx. 40 g | Salt: approx. 1.2 g

BEEF KEBABS WITH GARLIC YOGURT SAUCE

Juicy beef kebabs seasoned with Mediterranean spices and served with a refreshing garlic yogurt sauce. These kebabs are perfect for grilling and pair beautifully with rice or fresh salad.

Portions: 4 | **Difficulty Level:** Easy |
Preparation Time: 20 minutes (plus 30 minutes marinating time) |
Cooking Time: 10 minutes | **Total Time:** 1 hour

INGREDIENTS:

For the Kebabs:
- 500 g beef mince
- 1 small onion, finely chopped
- 2 cloves garlic, minced
- 1 tablespoon fresh parsley, chopped
- 1 teaspoon ground cumin
- 1 teaspoon ground coriander
- 1/2 teaspoon paprika
- 1/2 teaspoon ground cinnamon
- Salt and freshly ground black pepper to taste
- Wooden or metal skewers

For the Garlic Yogurt Sauce:
- 150 g Greek yogurt
- 1 clove garlic, minced
- 1 tablespoon lemon juice
- 1 tablespoon fresh mint, chopped
- Salt and freshly ground black pepper to taste

INSTRUCTIONS:

1. **Prepare the beef mixture:** In a large bowl, combine the beef mince, chopped onion, garlic, parsley, cumin, coriander, paprika, cinnamon, salt, and black pepper. Mix well with your hands until the ingredients are evenly combined.
2. **Form the kebabs:** Divide the beef mixture into 8 equal portions and shape each portion into a long sausage shape around a skewer. If using wooden skewers, soak them in water for 30 minutes beforehand to prevent burning.
3. **Marinate:** Place the kebabs in the refrigerator to marinate for at least 30 minutes to allow the flavors to develop.
4. **Grill the kebabs:** Preheat the grill or grill pan over medium-high heat. Grill the kebabs for 3-4 minutes on each side until cooked through and slightly charred.
5. **Prepare the garlic yogurt sauce:** In a small bowl, mix the Greek yogurt, minced garlic, lemon juice, mint, salt, and black pepper. Stir well and refrigerate until ready to serve.
6. **Serve:** Serve the beef kebabs hot, drizzled with garlic yogurt sauce. Pair with rice, couscous, or a fresh salad for a complete Mediterranean meal.

ESTIMATED NUTRITIONAL INFORMATION PER SERVING:
Calories: approx. 400 kcal | Fat: approx. 25 g | Carbohydrates: approx. 5 g |
Protein: approx. 35 g | Salt: approx. 1.0 g

GREEK-STYLE LAMB MEATBALLS WITH TZATZIKI

Tender lamb meatballs infused with Mediterranean herbs and spices, served with a refreshing homemade tzatziki sauce. These flavorful meatballs are perfect for a hearty main course, paired with pita bread or rice.

Portions: 4 | **Difficulty Level:** Medium | **Preparation Time:** 20 minutes | **Cooking Time:** 25 minutes | **Total Time:** 45 minutes

INGREDIENTS:

For the Meatballs:
- 500 g ground lamb
- 1 small onion, finely chopped
- 2 cloves garlic, minced
- 1 tablespoon fresh mint, chopped
- 1 tablespoon fresh parsley, chopped
- 1 teaspoon ground cumin
- 1 teaspoon dried oregano
- 1 egg, beaten
- 50 g breadcrumbs
- Salt and freshly ground black pepper to taste
- Olive oil for frying

For the Tzatziki:
- 200 g Greek yogurt
- 1/2 cucumber, grated and squeezed to remove excess water
- 1 clove garlic, minced
- 1 tablespoon lemon juice
- 1 tablespoon fresh dill, chopped
- Salt and freshly ground black pepper to taste

INSTRUCTIONS:

1. **Prepare the meatballs:** In a large bowl, combine the ground lamb, chopped onion, minced garlic, mint, parsley, cumin, oregano, egg, and breadcrumbs. Season with salt and black pepper. Mix the ingredients together until well combined.
2. **Shape the meatballs:** Using your hands, form the mixture into small meatballs, about 2-3 cm in diameter. Set the meatballs aside.
3. **Cook the meatballs:** Heat a large skillet over medium heat and add a drizzle of olive oil. Fry the meatballs in batches, turning occasionally, until browned on all sides and cooked through, about 10-12 minutes. Transfer the cooked meatballs to a plate lined with paper towels to drain excess oil.
4. **Prepare the tzatziki:** In a bowl, combine the Greek yogurt, grated cucumber, minced garlic, lemon juice, dill, salt, and black pepper. Mix well and refrigerate until ready to serve.
5. **Serve:** Serve the lamb meatballs with the tzatziki sauce on the side. These meatballs pair perfectly with warm pita bread, a fresh salad, or rice for a complete meal.

ESTIMATED NUTRITIONAL INFORMATION PER SERVING:
Calories: approx. 450 kcal | Fat: approx. 30 g | Carbohydrates: approx. 10 g | Protein: approx. 30 g | Salt: approx. 1.0 g

CHAPTER 7: DESSERTS

Light and fruity Mediterranean desserts that celebrate natural sweetness, local fruits, and Mediterranean flavours.

LEMON AND ALMOND CAKE WITH A HONEY DRIZZLE

A moist and zesty cake made with ground almonds and fresh lemon juice, finished with a sweet honey drizzle. A delightful and simple dessert.

Portions: 8 | **Difficulty Level:** Medium | **Preparation Time:** 15 minutes | **Cooking Time:** 35 minutes | **Total Time:** 50 minutes

INGREDIENTS:

- 200 g ground almonds
- 150 g caster sugar
- 3 eggs
- Zest and juice of 2 lemons
- 100 g unsalted butter, melted
- 1 teaspoon baking powder
- 2 tablespoons honey (for drizzling)
- A pinch of salt

INSTRUCTIONS:

1. **Preheat the oven:** Preheat your oven to 180°C (350°F). Grease and line a 20cm (8-inch) round cake tin with parchment paper.
2. **Prepare the cake batter:** In a large mixing bowl, whisk together the ground almonds, caster sugar, baking powder, and a pinch of salt. In a separate bowl, whisk the eggs until frothy, then add the lemon zest, lemon juice, and melted butter. Stir the wet ingredients into the dry ingredients until well combined.
3. **Bake the cake:** Pour the batter into the prepared cake tin and smooth the top. Bake in the preheated oven for 30-35 minutes, or until a toothpick inserted into the centre comes out clean. The cake should be golden brown and slightly springy to the touch.
4. **Drizzle with honey:** Remove the cake from the oven and let it cool slightly. While the cake is still warm, drizzle the honey evenly over the top. Allow the cake to cool completely before serving.
5. **Serve:** Slice and serve the lemon and almond cake with an extra drizzle of honey if desired. This cake pairs beautifully with a cup of tea or coffee for a light and zesty dessert.

ESTIMATED NUTRITIONAL INFORMATION PER SERVING:

Calories: approx. 280 kcal | Fat: approx. 18 g | Carbohydrates: approx. 24 g | Protein: approx. 6 g | Salt: approx. 0.2 g

ORANGE AND OLIVE OIL CAKE WITH A CITRUS GLAZE

This light and fragrant cake uses olive oil to create a moist texture, with a bright citrus glaze that makes it a refreshing end to any meal.

Portions: 8 | **Difficulty Level:** Medium | **Preparation Time:** 15 minutes | **Cooking Time:** 40 minutes | **Total Time:** 55 minutes

INGREDIENTS:

- 200 g plain flour
- 150 g caster sugar
- 3 large eggs
- 125 ml extra virgin olive oil
- Zest and juice of 1 large orange
- 1 teaspoon vanilla extract
- 1 teaspoon baking powder
- 1/2 teaspoon baking soda
- A pinch of salt

For the Citrus Glaze:
- Juice of 1 lemon
- 100 g icing sugar

INSTRUCTIONS:

1. **Preheat the oven:** Preheat your oven to 180°C (350°F). Grease and line a 20cm (8-inch) round cake tin with parchment paper.
2. **Prepare the cake batter:** In a large mixing bowl, whisk together the flour, baking powder, baking soda, and a pinch of salt. In a separate bowl, beat the eggs and caster sugar until light and fluffy. Slowly whisk in the olive oil, orange zest, orange juice, and vanilla extract.
3. **Combine wet and dry ingredients:** Gradually fold the dry ingredients into the wet mixture until fully incorporated. Be careful not to overmix.
4. **Bake the cake:** Pour the batter into the prepared cake tin and bake in the preheated oven for 35-40 minutes, or until a toothpick inserted into the centre comes out clean. The cake should be golden and have a slight spring when touched.
5. **Prepare the citrus glaze:** While the cake is baking, whisk together the lemon juice and icing sugar to create the glaze. Adjust the consistency by adding more icing sugar if needed.
6. **Glaze the cake:** Once the cake has cooled for 10-15 minutes, remove it from the tin and drizzle the citrus glaze over the top, allowing it to soak in.
7. **Serve:** Slice and serve the cake once fully cooled. This light and fragrant cake is perfect with a cup of tea or as a refreshing dessert after a meal.

ESTIMATED NUTRITIONAL INFORMATION PER SERVING:
Calories: approx. 300 kcal | Fat: approx. 15 g | Carbohydrates: approx. 35 g | Protein: approx. 4 g | Salt: approx. 0.2 g

FRESH BERRIES WITH GREEK YOGURT AND HONEY

A simple and healthy dessert, featuring fresh UK berries paired with creamy Greek yoghourt and a drizzle of honey. Perfect for a light, satisfying treat.

Portions: 4 | **Difficulty Level:** Easy | **Preparation Time:** 5 minutes | **Total Time:** 5 minutes

INGREDIENTS:

- 400 g mixed fresh berries (such as strawberries, raspberries, blueberries, and blackberries)
- 400 g Greek yoghourt
- 4 tablespoons honey
- 1 teaspoon vanilla extract (optional)
- Fresh mint leaves for garnish (optional)

INSTRUCTIONS:

1. **Prepare the yoghourt:** In a small bowl, stir the vanilla extract into the Greek yoghourt (if using). Divide the yoghourt evenly between 4 bowls.
2. **Assemble the dessert:** Top each serving of yoghourt with an equal portion of mixed fresh berries.
3. **Drizzle with honey:** Drizzle 1 tablespoon of honey over each bowl of berries and yoghourt. For extra flavour, use a floral honey such as wildflower or orange blossom.
4. **Serve:** Garnish with fresh mint leaves if desired. This simple and healthy dessert is perfect for a light, refreshing treat.

ESTIMATED NUTRITIONAL INFORMATION PER SERVING:
Calories: approx. 220 kcal | Fat: approx. 7 g | Carbohydrates: approx. 25 g | Protein: approx. 10 g | Salt: approx. 0.1 g

BAKLAVA WITH WALNUTS AND PISTACHIOS

Crispy layers of filo pastry filled with a mixture of spiced walnuts and pistachios, all soaked in a fragrant honey syrup. A rich and indulgent Mediterranean dessert.

Portions: 12 | **Difficulty Level:** Medium | **Preparation Time:** 30 minutes | **Cooking Time:** 45 minutes | **Total Time:** 1 hour 15 minutes

INGREDIENTS:

- 200 g walnuts, finely chopped
- 150 g pistachios, finely chopped
- 2 teaspoons ground cinnamon
- 300 g filo pastry (about 12 sheets)
- 150 g unsalted butter, melted

For the Syrup:
- 200 g sugar
- 120 ml water
- 120 ml honey
- 1 cinnamon stick
- 2 tablespoons lemon juice
- 1 tablespoon orange blossom water (optional)

INSTRUCTIONS:

1. **Preheat the oven:** Preheat your oven to 180°C (350°F). Grease a 23 x 33 cm (9 x 13 inch) baking dish with butter.
2. **Prepare the nut filling:** In a bowl, mix together the chopped walnuts, pistachios, and ground cinnamon. Set aside.
3. **Layer the filo pastry:** Lay one sheet of filo pastry in the bottom of the greased baking dish and brush lightly with melted butter. Repeat this process with 5 more sheets of filo, brushing each layer with butter.
4. **Add the nut filling:** Evenly spread half of the nut mixture over the filo layers. Add 4 more layers of filo on top, brushing each with butter. Spread the remaining nut mixture evenly. Top with the remaining 2 sheets of filo, brushing each with butter.
5. **Cut the baklava:** Using a sharp knife, cut the baklava into diamonds or squares.
6. **Bake the baklava:** Bake in the preheated oven for 40-45 minutes, or until the pastry is golden and crisp.
7. **Prepare the syrup:** While the baklava is baking, combine the sugar, water, honey, cinnamon stick, and lemon juice in a saucepan. Bring to a boil, then reduce heat and simmer for 10 minutes. Remove from heat and stir in the orange blossom water, if using. Let the syrup cool slightly.
8. **Add the syrup:** Once the baklava is done baking, remove it from the oven and immediately pour the warm syrup over the hot baklava, ensuring it soaks in evenly. Let the baklava cool completely before serving.
9. **Serve:** Once cooled, the baklava can be served.

ESTIMATED NUTRITIONAL INFORMATION PER SERVING:
Calories: approx. 350 kcal | Fat: approx. 20 g | Carbohydrates: approx. 35 g | Protein: approx. 5 g | Salt: approx. 0.2 g

RICOTTA AND HONEY TART WITH FRESH FIGS

A delicate tart made with creamy ricotta cheese, sweetened with honey and topped with slices of fresh figs for an elegant and light dessert.

Portions: 8 | **Difficulty Level:** Medium | **Preparation Time:** 20 minutes | **Cooking Time:** 30 minutes | **Total Time:** 50 minutes

INGREDIENTS:

- 200 g ricotta cheese
- 100 g cream cheese, softened
- 2 large eggs
- 3 tablespoons honey
- 1 teaspoon vanilla extract
- 1 tablespoon lemon zest
- 6-8 fresh figs, halved

For the Tart Crust:
- 200 g plain flour
- 100 g unsalted butter, cold and cubed
- 50 g icing sugar
- 1 egg yolk
- 1-2 tablespoons cold water

INSTRUCTIONS:

1. **Prepare the tart crust:** In a food processor, pulse the flour, cold butter, and icing sugar until the mixture resembles coarse breadcrumbs. Add the egg yolk and 1 tablespoon of cold water, pulsing until the dough just comes together. Add more water if needed. Form the dough into a ball, wrap in cling film, and refrigerate for 30 minutes.
2. **Preheat the oven:** Preheat your oven to 180°C (350°F). Roll out the dough on a lightly floured surface and line a 23cm (9-inch) tart tin. Prick the base with a fork and chill for 10 minutes. Line the crust with baking paper and fill with baking beans or rice. Bake for 10 minutes, then remove the baking paper and beans, and bake for another 5-7 minutes until lightly golden. Set aside to cool.
3. **Prepare the filling:** In a mixing bowl, whisk together the ricotta, cream cheese, eggs, honey, vanilla extract, and lemon zest until smooth and creamy.
4. **Assemble the tart:** Pour the ricotta mixture into the cooled tart crust and smooth the top. Arrange the halved fresh figs on top of the filling.
5. **Bake the tart:** Bake in the preheated oven for 25-30 minutes, or until the filling is set and slightly golden around the edges. Remove from the oven and let cool.
6. **Serve:** Drizzle with additional honey before serving if desired. This elegant tart is perfect as a light and refreshing dessert.

ESTIMATED NUTRITIONAL INFORMATION PER SERVING:
Calories: approx. 320 kcal | Fat: approx. 18 g | Carbohydrates: approx. 30 g | Protein: approx. 8 g | Salt: approx. 0.2 g

POACHED PEARS IN RED WINE WITH CINNAMON AND STAR ANISE

Tender pears poached in a rich red wine sauce, infused with cinnamon and star anise for a fragrant and warming dessert.

Portions: 4 | **Difficulty Level:** Easy | **Preparation Time:** 10 minutes | **Cooking Time:** 30 minutes | **Total Time:** 40 minutes

INGREDIENTS:

- 4 ripe but firm pears, peeled and cored
- 750 ml red wine (such as Merlot or Shiraz)
- 150 g sugar
- 1 cinnamon stick
- 2 star anise
- Zest of 1 orange
- 1 vanilla pod, split (or 1 teaspoon vanilla extract)

INSTRUCTIONS:

1. **Prepare the poaching liquid:** In a large saucepan, combine the red wine, sugar, cinnamon stick, star anise, orange zest, and vanilla pod. Bring the mixture to a gentle simmer over medium heat, stirring occasionally to dissolve the sugar.
2. **Poach the pears:** Carefully lower the peeled pears into the simmering wine mixture. Cover and simmer gently for 25-30 minutes, turning the pears occasionally, until they are tender but not falling apart. The pears should take on a deep red colour from the wine.
3. **Remove the pears:** Using a slotted spoon, remove the pears from the poaching liquid and set aside.
4. **Reduce the poaching liquid:** Increase the heat and bring the remaining wine mixture to a boil. Let it reduce for about 10-15 minutes until it becomes a syrupy consistency.
5. **Serve:** Place each poached pear in a serving dish and drizzle with the reduced red wine syrup. These fragrant pears can be served warm or chilled, and pair beautifully with vanilla ice cream or a dollop of whipped cream.

ESTIMATED NUTRITIONAL INFORMATION PER SERVING:
Calories: approx. 250 kcal | Fat: approx. 0 g | Carbohydrates: approx. 50 g | Protein: approx. 1 g | Salt: approx. 0.1 g

LEMON SORBET WITH FRESH MINT

A refreshing lemon sorbet, perfect for cleansing the palate after a meal. The addition of fresh mint brings an extra layer of freshness.

Portions: 4 | **Difficulty Level:** Easy | **Preparation Time:** 10 minutes (plus freezing time) | **Cooking Time:** 5 minutes | **Total Time:** 15 minutes (plus freezing)

INGREDIENTS:

- 200 g sugar
- 250 ml water
- 250 ml freshly squeezed lemon juice (about 4-5 lemons)
- Zest of 1 lemon
- Fresh mint leaves for garnish

INSTRUCTIONS:

1. **Make the syrup:** In a small saucepan, combine the sugar and water. Bring to a simmer over medium heat, stirring occasionally until the sugar dissolves completely. Remove from heat and allow the syrup to cool to room temperature.
2. **Prepare the sorbet mixture:** Once the syrup has cooled, stir in the freshly squeezed lemon juice and lemon zest. Mix well.
3. **Freeze the sorbet:** Pour the lemon mixture into an ice cream maker and churn according to the manufacturer's instructions until the sorbet reaches a smooth, frozen consistency. If you don't have an ice cream maker, pour the mixture into a shallow dish and place it in the freezer, stirring every 30 minutes until it is fully frozen (about 3-4 hours).
4. **Serve:** Scoop the lemon sorbet into serving bowls or glasses and garnish with fresh mint leaves. This refreshing sorbet is perfect as a palate cleanser or light dessert.

ESTIMATED NUTRITIONAL INFORMATION PER SERVING:
Calories: approx. 160 kcal | Fat: 0 g | Carbohydrates: approx. 40 g | Protein: approx. 0 g | Salt: approx. 0.1 g

PISTACHIO AND ROSEWATER ICE CREAM

Creamy pistachio ice cream with a delicate hint of rosewater, making for a unique and delightful Mediterranean treat.

Portions: 4 | **Difficulty Level:** Medium | **Preparation Time:** 15 minutes (plus freezing time) | **Cooking Time:** 5 minutes | **Total Time:** 20 minutes (plus freezing)

INGREDIENTS:
- 250 ml whole milk
- 250 ml heavy cream
- 100 g sugar
- 3 large egg yolks
- 1 teaspoon rosewater (adjust to taste)
- 100 g pistachios, finely chopped (plus extra for garnish)

INSTRUCTIONS:
1. **Heat the milk and cream:** In a medium saucepan, combine the milk and cream. Heat gently over medium heat until the mixture just begins to simmer, then remove from heat.
2. **Whisk the egg yolks and sugar:** In a separate bowl, whisk together the egg yolks and sugar until pale and smooth.
3. **Temper the eggs:** Slowly pour a small amount of the warm milk mixture into the egg yolk mixture, whisking constantly to prevent curdling. Gradually whisk in the rest of the warm milk mixture.
4. **Cook the custard:** Return the custard mixture to the saucepan and cook over low heat, stirring constantly, until the mixture thickens and coats the back of a spoon. Remove from heat and stir in the rosewater.
5. **Cool and freeze the mixture:** Allow the custard to cool to room temperature, then refrigerate for at least 2 hours or until chilled. Once chilled, churn the mixture in an ice cream maker according to the manufacturer's instructions. Add the chopped pistachios during the last few minutes of churning.
6. **Freeze and serve:** Transfer the ice cream to a container and freeze for an additional 2-3 hours, or until firm. Serve scoops of pistachio and rosewater ice cream garnished with extra chopped pistachios.

ESTIMATED NUTRITIONAL INFORMATION PER SERVING:
Calories: approx. 320 kcal | Fat: approx. 22 g | Carbohydrates: approx. 25 g | Protein: approx. 6 g | Salt: approx. 0.1 g

ALMOND BISCOTTI WITH A HINT OF LEMON ZEST

Crunchy biscotti flavoured with almond and a touch of lemon zest, perfect for dipping in coffee or tea.

Portions: 24 biscotti | **Difficulty Level:** Medium | **Preparation Time:** 15 minutes | **Cooking Time:** 45 minutes | **Total Time:** 1 hour

INGREDIENTS:

- 250 g plain flour
- 150 g sugar
- 1 teaspoon baking powder
- 1/2 teaspoon salt
- 2 large eggs
- 1 teaspoon vanilla extract
- Zest of 1 lemon
- 150 g whole almonds, toasted
- 50 g slivered almonds for garnish (optional)

INSTRUCTIONS:

1. **Preheat the oven:** Preheat your oven to 180°C (350°F). Line a baking sheet with parchment paper.
2. **Prepare the dry ingredients:** In a large mixing bowl, whisk together the flour, sugar, baking powder, and salt. Stir in the lemon zest and toasted whole almonds.
3. **Prepare the wet ingredients:** In a separate bowl, whisk together the eggs and vanilla extract. Add the wet ingredients to the dry ingredients and stir until a dough forms. The dough will be slightly sticky.
4. **Shape the dough:** Turn the dough onto a floured surface and divide it in half. Shape each half into a log about 25 cm (10 inches) long and 5 cm (2 inches) wide. Place the logs on the prepared baking sheet.
5. **First bake:** Bake the logs in the preheated oven for 25-30 minutes, or until golden brown. Remove from the oven and allow the logs to cool for 10 minutes.
6. **Slice and second bake:** Reduce the oven temperature to 150°C (300°F). Using a sharp knife, slice the logs diagonally into 1.5 cm (1/2-inch) thick biscotti. Arrange the slices on the baking sheet, cut-side down, and bake for an additional 10-12 minutes on each side, until crisp and golden.
7. **Cool and serve:** Transfer the biscotti to a wire rack to cool completely. These almond biscotti, with a hint of lemon zest, are perfect for dipping in coffee or tea.

ESTIMATED NUTRITIONAL INFORMATION PER BISCOTTI:

Calories: approx. 100 kcal | Fat: approx. 4 g | Carbohydrates: approx. 15 g | Protein: approx. 2 g | Salt: approx. 0.1 g

STUFFED DATES WITH ALMONDS AND ORANGE BLOSSOM WATER

Sweet dates filled with almonds and a touch of fragrant orange blossom water, a simple yet exotic Mediterranean dessert.

Portions: 12 | **Difficulty Level:** Easy | **Preparation Time:** 10 minutes | **Total Time:** 10 minutes

INGREDIENTS:
- 12 Medjool dates, pitted
- 12 whole almonds, toasted
- 2 tablespoons orange blossom water
- 1 teaspoon honey (optional)
- Fresh orange zest, for garnish
- Ground pistachios, for garnish (optional)

INSTRUCTIONS:
1. **Prepare the dates:** Gently slice the dates lengthwise on one side and remove the pits, keeping the dates intact.
2. **Stuff the dates:** Place one toasted almond inside each date.
3. **Add the orange blossom water:** Drizzle a small amount of orange blossom water inside each stuffed date. For added sweetness, you can drizzle a touch of honey over the top of the dates.
4. **Garnish:** Sprinkle fresh orange zest and, if desired, a pinch of ground pistachios over the stuffed dates for an extra layer of flavour and texture.
5. **Serve:** Arrange the stuffed dates on a serving platter. These stuffed dates make for an easy yet exotic Mediterranean dessert or snack.

ESTIMATED NUTRITIONAL INFORMATION PER DATE:
Calories: approx. 90 kcal | Fat: approx. 3 g | Carbohydrates: approx. 15 g | Protein: approx. 1 g | Salt: approx. 0 g

CHAPTER 8: PRESERVES, SAUCES, AND CONDIMENTS

> Homemade sauces, dips, and condiments to accompany your meals or use in other recipes.

OLIVE TAPENADE

A rich and briny spread made from black olives, capers, and anchovies. Perfect for spreading on toast or serving as part of a mezze platter.

Portions: 4 | **Difficulty Level:** Easy | **Preparation Time:** 10 minutes | **Total Time:** 10 minutes

INGREDIENTS:
- 200 g black olives, pitted
- 1 tablespoon capers, rinsed
- 3 anchovy fillets (optional)
- 2 cloves garlic, minced
- 2 tablespoons extra virgin olive oil
- 1 tablespoon fresh lemon juice
- 1 tablespoon fresh parsley, chopped
- Salt and freshly ground black pepper to taste

INSTRUCTIONS:
1. **Prepare the tapenade:** In a food processor, combine the black olives, capers, anchovy fillets (if using), and minced garlic. Pulse a few times until coarsely chopped.
2. **Add the olive oil and lemon:** With the food processor running, slowly drizzle in the olive oil and lemon juice until the mixture forms a chunky paste. Be careful not to over-process—you want the tapenade to have some texture.
3. **Season:** Stir in the chopped parsley and season with salt and freshly ground black pepper to taste.
4. **Serve:** Transfer the tapenade to a serving bowl and serve with toasted bread, crackers, or as part of a mezze platter. This rich and flavorful spread is also great for topping grilled meats or vegetables.

ESTIMATED NUTRITIONAL INFORMATION PER SERVING:
Calories: approx. 120 kcal | Fat: approx. 10 g | Carbohydrates: approx. 5 g | Protein: approx. 1 g | Salt: approx. 0.8 g

PRESERVED LEMONS

Tart and salty preserved lemons are a key ingredient in many Mediterranean dishes. These can be used in tagines, salads, or dressings to add a bright, citrusy flavour.

Portions: 1 jar (about 4 preserved lemons) | **Difficulty Level:** Easy | **Preparation Time:** 10 minutes | **Curing Time:** 4 weeks | **Total Time:** 4 weeks and 10 minutes

INGREDIENTS:
- 4 medium lemons, scrubbed clean
- 4 tablespoons sea salt
- 2 additional lemons, juiced
- 1 cinnamon stick (optional)
- 2 bay leaves (optional)
- 4-5 whole black peppercorns (optional)
- Sterilised jar with a tight-fitting lid

INSTRUCTIONS:
1. **Prepare the lemons:** Slice the lemons lengthwise into quarters, leaving the bottom 1 cm (1/2 inch) of the lemon intact so the quarters are still connected.
2. **Salt the lemons:** Open each lemon slightly and pack the inside with 1 tablespoon of sea salt. Close the lemon and place it in the sterilised jar. Repeat with the remaining lemons, pressing them down to fit tightly in the jar.
3. **Add the lemon juice and spices:** Pour the juice of the additional 2 lemons into the jar to cover the salted lemons. If needed, add more lemon juice to ensure the lemons are fully submerged. Add the cinnamon stick, bay leaves, and black peppercorns, if using, for extra flavour.
4. **Seal the jar:** Tightly seal the jar with a lid and store it in a cool, dark place. Let the lemons cure for at least 4 weeks, shaking the jar occasionally to redistribute the salt and liquid.
5. **Use the preserved lemons:** Once cured, the lemons will be soft and ready to use. Rinse off excess salt before using, and use the rind in tagines, salads, dressings, or marinades for a bright, citrusy flavour.

ESTIMATED NUTRITIONAL INFORMATION PER LEMON (AFTER PRESERVING):
Calories: approx. 15 kcal | Fat: 0 g | Carbohydrates: approx. 5 g | Protein: 0 g | Salt: approx. 2.0 g

HARISSA PASTE

A spicy, flavorful paste made with roasted red peppers, chilies, and garlic. Ideal for adding a kick to meats, vegetables, or sauces.

Portions: 1 small jar (about 200 g) | **Difficulty Level:** Medium | **Preparation Time:** 20 minutes | **Total Time:** 20 minutes

INGREDIENTS:

- 4 large dried red chilies, seeds removed
- 2 roasted red peppers, peeled and chopped
- 3 cloves garlic, minced
- 1 teaspoon ground cumin
- 1 teaspoon ground coriander
- 1 teaspoon ground caraway seeds
- 1 tablespoon tomato paste
- 3 tablespoons olive oil
- 1 tablespoon fresh lemon juice
- Salt to taste

INSTRUCTIONS:

1. **Soak the chilies:** Place the dried red chilies in a bowl of hot water and soak for about 10-15 minutes until softened. Drain the chilies and roughly chop them.
2. **Blend the ingredients:** In a food processor, combine the soaked chilies, roasted red peppers, minced garlic, cumin, coriander, caraway seeds, tomato paste, and olive oil. Blend until smooth, adding more olive oil if needed to reach your desired consistency.
3. **Season the harissa:** Stir in the fresh lemon juice and season with salt to taste. Blend again to fully incorporate the flavours.
4. **Store:** Transfer the harissa paste to a sterilised jar and drizzle a little extra olive oil on top to preserve it. Seal the jar and store in the refrigerator for up to 2 weeks.
5. **Serve:** Use harissa as a marinade for meats, mix it into sauces, or spread it on sandwiches for a spicy and flavorful kick. This versatile paste adds depth and heat to a wide variety of dishes.

ESTIMATED NUTRITIONAL INFORMATION PER TABLESPOON:
Calories: approx. 50 kcal | Fat: approx. 4 g | Carbohydrates: approx. 4 g | Protein: approx. 1 g | Salt: approx. 0.2 g

HOMEMADE TZATZIKI

A cool and creamy yoghourt-based dip, flavoured with fresh cucumber, garlic, and dill. A perfect accompaniment for grilled meats or vegetables.

Portions: 4 | **Difficulty Level:** Easy | **Preparation Time:** 10 minutes | **Total Time:** 10 minutes

INGREDIENTS:

- 250 g Greek yoghourt
- 1/2 cucumber, grated and squeezed to remove excess water
- 2 cloves garlic, minced
- 1 tablespoon olive oil
- 1 tablespoon lemon juice
- 1 tablespoon fresh dill, chopped
- Salt and freshly ground black pepper to taste

INSTRUCTIONS:

1. **Prepare the cucumber:** Grate the cucumber using a box grater and place it in a clean kitchen towel. Squeeze out as much excess water as possible to prevent the tzatziki from becoming too watery.
2. **Mix the ingredients:** In a bowl, combine the Greek yoghourt, grated cucumber, minced garlic, olive oil, lemon juice, and chopped dill. Stir well to combine.
3. **Season:** Add salt and freshly ground black pepper to taste, adjusting the seasoning as needed.
4. **Serve:** Serve the tzatziki chilled, garnished with a drizzle of olive oil and a sprig of dill if desired. This creamy and refreshing dip pairs perfectly with grilled meats, vegetables, or warm pita bread.

ESTIMATED NUTRITIONAL INFORMATION PER SERVING:
Calories: approx. 100 kcal | Fat: approx. 7 g | Carbohydrates: approx. 4 g | Protein: approx. 5 g | Salt: approx. 0.4 g

POMEGRANATE MOLASSES

A thick and tangy syrup made from reduced pomegranate juice, used in dressings and marinades for a burst of sweet and sour flavour.

Portions: 1 small jar (about 200 ml) | **Difficulty Level:** Easy | **Preparation Time:** 5 minutes | **Cooking Time:** 1 hour | **Total Time:** 1 hour 5 minutes

INGREDIENTS:
- 500 ml pomegranate juice (fresh or store-bought)
- 100 g sugar
- 2 tablespoons lemon juice

INSTRUCTIONS:
1. **Prepare the mixture:** In a medium saucepan, combine the pomegranate juice, sugar, and lemon juice. Stir to dissolve the sugar.
2. **Simmer the mixture:** Bring the mixture to a boil over medium heat, then reduce the heat to low and let it simmer gently. Stir occasionally and cook for about 45 minutes to 1 hour, or until the liquid has reduced by about two-thirds and has a thick, syrupy consistency.
3. **Cool and store:** Remove the saucepan from the heat and allow the pomegranate molasses to cool completely. The syrup will thicken further as it cools. Transfer to a sterilised jar and store in the refrigerator for up to 6 months.
4. **Use:** Pomegranate molasses is a versatile ingredient that can be used in salad dressings, marinades, sauces, or even drizzled over roasted vegetables and grilled meats. It adds a sweet, tangy depth to many Mediterranean dishes.

ESTIMATED NUTRITIONAL INFORMATION PER TABLESPOON:
Calories: approx. 60 kcal | Fat: 0 g | Carbohydrates: approx. 15 g | Protein: 0 g | Salt: approx. 0 g

TOMATO AND RED PEPPER RELISH

A sweet and tangy relish made with ripe tomatoes and red peppers, perfect for pairing with grilled meats or as a spread for sandwiches.

Portions: 1 jar (about 250 ml) | **Difficulty Level:** Easy | **Preparation Time:** 10 minutes | **Cooking Time:** 45 minutes | **Total Time:** 55 minutes

INGREDIENTS:
- 4 large ripe tomatoes, chopped
- 2 large red bell peppers, chopped
- 1 small onion, finely chopped
- 2 cloves garlic, minced
- 2 tablespoons olive oil
- 2 tablespoons red wine vinegar
- 1 tablespoon sugar
- 1 teaspoon smoked paprika
- Salt and freshly ground black pepper to taste

INSTRUCTIONS:
1. **Sauté the vegetables:** In a large saucepan, heat the olive oil over medium heat. Add the chopped onion and garlic and sauté for 3-4 minutes until softened.
2. **Cook the tomatoes and peppers:** Add the chopped tomatoes, red bell peppers, red wine vinegar, sugar, smoked paprika, salt, and pepper. Stir to combine and bring the mixture to a simmer.
3. **Simmer the relish:** Reduce the heat to low and let the mixture simmer gently for about 40-45 minutes, stirring occasionally, until the vegetables have softened and the relish has thickened to your desired consistency.
4. **Cool and store:** Once cooked, remove the saucepan from the heat and let the relish cool to room temperature. Transfer to a sterilised jar and store in the refrigerator for up to 2 weeks.
5. **Serve:** Use this sweet and tangy tomato and red pepper relish as a topping for grilled meats, a spread for sandwiches, or even as a dip. It adds a burst of flavour to a variety of dishes.

ESTIMATED NUTRITIONAL INFORMATION PER TABLESPOON:
Calories: approx. 20 kcal | Fat: approx. 1 g | Carbohydrates: approx. 3 g | Protein: approx. 0.5 g | Salt: approx. 0.2 g

ROMESCO SAUCE

A smoky and nutty sauce made with roasted red peppers, almonds, and garlic, ideal for serving with vegetables or seafood.

Portions: 1 jar (about 250 ml) | **Difficulty Level:** Medium | **Preparation Time:** 15 minutes | **Cooking Time:** 10 minutes | **Total Time:** 25 minutes

INGREDIENTS:
- 2 large roasted red peppers, peeled and chopped
- 50 g blanched almonds, toasted
- 2 cloves garlic, minced
- 1 tablespoon tomato paste
- 1 tablespoon red wine vinegar
- 1 teaspoon smoked paprika
- 50 ml olive oil
- Salt and freshly ground black pepper to taste
- 1 slice of stale bread, toasted (optional)

INSTRUCTIONS:
1. **Toast the almonds:** In a dry skillet over medium heat, toast the almonds for 3-4 minutes, stirring frequently until golden and fragrant. Remove from heat and let cool.
2. **Blend the ingredients:** In a food processor, combine the roasted red peppers, toasted almonds, garlic, tomato paste, red wine vinegar, smoked paprika, and toasted bread (if using). Pulse until the mixture is coarsely chopped.
3. **Add the olive oil:** With the food processor running, slowly drizzle in the olive oil until the sauce is smooth and creamy. Season with salt and freshly ground black pepper to taste.
4. **Serve:** Romesco sauce is perfect for serving with grilled vegetables, seafood, or meats. It can also be used as a dip or spread. Its smoky and nutty flavour makes it a versatile and delicious condiment.
5. **Store:** Transfer the romesco sauce to a sterilised jar and store in the refrigerator for up to 1 week.

ESTIMATED NUTRITIONAL INFORMATION PER TABLESPOON:
Calories: approx. 70 kcal | Fat: approx. 6 g | Carbohydrates: approx. 2 g | Protein: approx. 1 g | Salt: approx. 0.1 g

BASIL PESTO WITH WALNUTS

A fresh and vibrant pesto made with basil, walnuts, garlic, and olive oil, perfect for tossing with pasta or spreading on sandwiches.

Portions: 1 small jar (about 200 ml) | **Difficulty Level:** Easy | **Preparation Time:** 10 minutes | **Total Time:** 10 minutes

INGREDIENTS:

- 100 g fresh basil leaves
- 50 g walnuts, toasted
- 2 cloves garlic, minced
- 50 g Parmesan cheese, grated
- 100 ml extra virgin olive oil
- 1 tablespoon fresh lemon juice
- Salt and freshly ground black pepper to taste

INSTRUCTIONS:

1. **Toast the walnuts:** In a dry skillet over medium heat, toast the walnuts for 3-4 minutes until golden and fragrant. Remove from heat and let cool.
2. **Blend the ingredients:** In a food processor, combine the basil leaves, toasted walnuts, minced garlic, Parmesan cheese, and lemon juice. Pulse until coarsely chopped.
3. **Add the olive oil:** With the food processor running, slowly drizzle in the olive oil until the pesto reaches your desired consistency. You can add more olive oil if needed. Season with salt and freshly ground black pepper to taste.
4. **Serve:** This fresh and vibrant basil pesto with walnuts is perfect for tossing with pasta, spreading on sandwiches, or using as a dip. It adds a burst of flavour to any dish.
5. **Store:** Transfer the pesto to a sterilised jar and store in the refrigerator for up to 1 week. Cover the top with a layer of olive oil to preserve freshness.

ESTIMATED NUTRITIONAL INFORMATION PER TABLESPOON:
Calories: approx. 100 kcal | Fat: approx. 10 g | Carbohydrates: approx. 1 g | Protein: approx. 2 g | Salt: approx. 0.1 g

GARLIC AIOLI WITH LEMON

A creamy garlic aioli with a hint of lemon, perfect for dipping fries or as a spread for sandwiches and wraps.

Portions: 1 small jar (about 200 ml) | **Difficulty Level:** Easy | **Preparation Time:** 10 minutes | **Total Time:** 10 minutes

INGREDIENTS:
- 2 large egg yolks
- 3 cloves garlic, minced
- 1 tablespoon Dijon mustard
- 1 tablespoon fresh lemon juice
- 200 ml extra virgin olive oil
- Salt and freshly ground black pepper to taste

INSTRUCTIONS:
1. **Whisk the base:** In a medium bowl, whisk together the egg yolks, minced garlic, Dijon mustard, and lemon juice until smooth.
2. **Add the olive oil:** Slowly drizzle in the olive oil while whisking continuously until the mixture thickens and emulsifies into a creamy aioli. If the mixture becomes too thick, add a little water to thin it out.
3. **Season:** Season the aioli with salt and freshly ground black pepper to taste. Adjust the lemon juice for extra tang if desired.
4. **Serve:** This creamy garlic aioli with a hint of lemon is perfect as a dip for fries, a spread for sandwiches, or a sauce for grilled vegetables and meats. Its rich and tangy flavour complements a wide variety of dishes.
5. **Store:** Transfer the aioli to a sterilised jar and store in the refrigerator for up to 1 week.

ESTIMATED NUTRITIONAL INFORMATION PER TABLESPOON:
Calories: approx. 90 kcal | Fat: approx. 10 g | Carbohydrates: approx. 0.5 g | Protein: approx. 0.5 g | Salt: approx. 0.1 g

TAHINI DRESSING WITH LEMON AND GARLIC

A smooth and rich tahini dressing, flavoured with lemon and garlic, ideal for drizzling over salads or roasted vegetables.

Portions: 1 small jar (about 200 ml) | **Difficulty Level:** Easy | **Preparation Time:** 5 minutes | **Total Time:** 5 minutes

INGREDIENTS:
- 100 g tahini (sesame paste)
- 2 tablespoons fresh lemon juice
- 1 clove garlic, minced
- 1 tablespoon olive oil
- 100 ml water (adjust for desired consistency)
- Salt and freshly ground black pepper to taste
- Fresh parsley, chopped (optional for garnish)

INSTRUCTIONS:
1. **Mix the ingredients:** In a bowl, whisk together the tahini, lemon juice, minced garlic, olive oil, and water. Whisk until smooth and creamy, adding more water if you prefer a thinner consistency.
2. **Season:** Add salt and freshly ground black pepper to taste. Adjust the seasoning and lemon juice as needed to balance the flavours.
3. **Serve:** This smooth and tangy tahini dressing is perfect for drizzling over salads, roasted vegetables, or grain bowls. It can also be used as a dip for pita bread or fresh veggies.
4. **Store:** Transfer the tahini dressing to a sterilised jar and store in the refrigerator for up to 1 week. Stir well before using, as the dressing may thicken slightly when chilled.

ESTIMATED NUTRITIONAL INFORMATION PER TABLESPOON:
Calories: approx. 70 kcal | Fat: approx. 6 g | Carbohydrates: approx. 2 g | Protein: approx. 2 g | Salt: approx. 0.1 g

SPICY RED PEPPER HUMMUS

A smoky and flavorful hummus, enhanced with roasted red pepper and a hint of spice. Perfect as a dip or spread for sandwiches, vegetables, or pita bread.

Portions: 4 | **Difficulty Level:** Easy | **Preparation Time:** 10 minutes | **Total Time:** 10 minutes

INGREDIENTS:

- 1 can (400 g) chickpeas, drained and rinsed
- 1 large roasted red pepper, chopped
- 2 tablespoons tahini
- 2 tablespoons olive oil
- 1 tablespoon lemon juice
- 1 garlic clove, minced
- 1 teaspoon smoked paprika
- 1/2 teaspoon ground cumin
- 1/2 teaspoon cayenne pepper (optional, for extra spice)
- Salt and freshly ground black pepper to taste

INSTRUCTIONS:

1. **Blend the ingredients:** In a food processor, combine the chickpeas, roasted red pepper, tahini, olive oil, lemon juice, garlic, smoked paprika, cumin, and cayenne pepper (if using). Blend until smooth, scraping down the sides as needed.
2. **Adjust consistency:** If the hummus is too thick, add a tablespoon or two of water or more olive oil until the desired consistency is reached.
3. **Season:** Taste and season with salt and freshly ground black pepper to your liking.
4. **Serve:** Spoon the spicy red pepper hummus into a serving bowl and drizzle with a little extra olive oil. Garnish with a sprinkle of smoked paprika or chopped fresh parsley. Serve with pita bread, crackers, or fresh vegetables for dipping.

ESTIMATED NUTRITIONAL INFORMATION PER SERVING:
Calories: approx. 200 kcal | Fat: approx. 12 g | Carbohydrates: approx. 20 g | Protein: approx. 5 g | Salt: approx. 0.5 g

ROASTED GARLIC AND HERB BUTTER

A creamy and flavorful butter infused with roasted garlic and fresh herbs, perfect for spreading on warm bread, melting over grilled meats, or adding to roasted vegetables.

Portions: 4 | **Difficulty Level:** Easy | **Preparation Time:** 10 minutes | **Cooking Time:** 30 minutes (for roasting garlic) | **Total Time:** 40 minutes

INGREDIENTS:

- 100 g unsalted butter, softened
- 1 head of garlic
- 1 tablespoon fresh parsley, chopped
- 1 tablespoon fresh thyme, chopped
- 1 tablespoon fresh chives, chopped
- 1 tablespoon olive oil
- Salt and freshly ground black pepper to taste

INSTRUCTIONS:

1. **Roast the garlic:** Preheat the oven to 180°C (350°F). Slice the top off the head of garlic, drizzle with olive oil, and wrap it in foil. Roast in the oven for 30 minutes until soft and golden. Let it cool slightly.
2. **Mix the butter:** In a small bowl, squeeze the roasted garlic cloves out of their skins and mash them into a paste. Add the softened butter, chopped parsley, thyme, and chives. Mix until well combined.
3. **Season:** Season the butter with salt and freshly ground black pepper to taste.
4. **Serve:** Spread the garlic and herb butter on warm bread, or use it to top grilled meats or vegetables. You can also shape the butter into a log and refrigerate it for future use.

ESTIMATED NUTRITIONAL INFORMATION PER SERVING:
Calories: approx. 180 kcal | Fat: approx. 18 g | Carbohydrates: approx. 2 g | Protein: approx. 1 g | Salt: approx. 0.3 g

CHILI OIL WITH GARLIC AND HERBS

A fragrant and spicy chili oil infused with garlic, rosemary, and thyme, perfect for drizzling over pizza, pasta, or roasted vegetables for an extra kick of flavor.

Portions: 1 small bottle (about 250 ml) | **Difficulty Level:** Easy | **Preparation Time:** 5 minutes | **Cooking Time:** 10 minutes | **Total Time:** 15 minutes

INGREDIENTS:

- 250 ml olive oil
- 2 teaspoons crushed red chili flakes
- 3 cloves garlic, sliced
- 1 sprig fresh rosemary
- 1 sprig fresh thyme
- 1 teaspoon smoked paprika (optional)
- Salt to taste

INSTRUCTIONS:

1. **Heat the oil:** In a small saucepan, combine the olive oil, garlic, rosemary, and thyme. Heat over low heat for about 5 minutes until the garlic becomes fragrant and starts to turn golden. Do not let the garlic burn.
2. **Add the spices:** Remove the saucepan from the heat and stir in the crushed red chili flakes, smoked paprika (if using), and salt. Let the oil cool completely, allowing the flavors to infuse.
3. **Strain the oil (optional):** For a smoother oil, strain the garlic, herbs, and chili flakes from the oil using a fine mesh sieve. Otherwise, leave them in for extra flavor and texture.
4. **Store:** Transfer the chili oil to a sterilized bottle or jar. Store in a cool, dark place for up to 1 month. Shake before each use.
5. **Serve:** Drizzle the chili oil over pizza, pasta, grilled meats, or roasted vegetables for an extra layer of heat and flavor.

ESTIMATED NUTRITIONAL INFORMATION PER TABLESPOON:
Calories: approx. 120 kcal | Fat: approx. 14 g | Carbohydrates: approx. 0.5 g | Protein: 0 g | Salt: approx. 0.1 g

SUN-DRIED TOMATO PESTO

A rich and flavorful pesto made with sun-dried tomatoes, garlic, and basil. Perfect for tossing with pasta, spreading on sandwiches, or using as a dip.

Portions: 1 small jar (about 200 ml) | **Difficulty Level:** Easy | **Preparation Time:** 10 minutes | **Total Time:** 10 minutes

INGREDIENTS:

- 100 g sun-dried tomatoes (in oil), drained
- 50 g Parmesan cheese, grated
- 50 g walnuts or pine nuts, toasted
- 2 cloves garlic, minced
- 1 handful fresh basil leaves
- 50 ml olive oil (plus more if needed)
- 1 tablespoon balsamic vinegar
- Salt and freshly ground black pepper to taste

INSTRUCTIONS:

1. **Blend the ingredients:** In a food processor, combine the sun-dried tomatoes, Parmesan cheese, walnuts or pine nuts, garlic, and basil. Pulse until the ingredients are finely chopped.
2. **Add olive oil and balsamic:** With the food processor running, slowly drizzle in the olive oil and balsamic vinegar until the mixture becomes smooth and creamy. You can add more olive oil if the pesto is too thick.
3. **Season:** Taste and season with salt and freshly ground black pepper to your liking.
4. **Serve:** This sun-dried tomato pesto is perfect for tossing with pasta, spreading on sandwiches, or using as a dip for bread. It also works great as a topping for grilled meats or vegetables.
5. **Store:** Transfer the pesto to a sterilized jar and store in the refrigerator for up to 1 week. Cover the top with a layer of olive oil to preserve freshness.

ESTIMATED NUTRITIONAL INFORMATION PER TABLESPOON:
Calories: approx. 90 kcal | Fat: approx. 7 g | Carbohydrates: approx. 3 g | Protein: approx. 2 g | Salt: approx. 0.2 g

DISCLAIMER

The information provided in *The XXL Mediterranean Diet Recipes Book* is intended for general informational purposes only and is not a substitute for professional medical advice, diagnosis, or treatment. Always consult your healthcare provider or a registered dietitian before making any significant changes to your diet, especially if you have pre-existing medical conditions or dietary restrictions. The nutritional information provided is an estimate and may vary based on ingredient brands, portion sizes, and preparation methods. The authors and publishers are not responsible for any adverse effects resulting from the use of the recipes or information contained in this book. Individual results may vary.

EXCLUSIVE BONUS

40 Weight Loss Recipes

&

14 Days Meal Plan

Scan the QR-Code and receive the FREE download:

Printed in Great Britain
by Amazon